COMPUTER SCIENCE, TECHNOLOGY AND APPLICATIONS

FEDERAL CYBERSECURITY

STRATEGY AND IMPLEMENTATION FOR RESEARCH AND DEVELOPMENT

COMPUTER SCIENCE, TECHNOLOGY AND APPLICATIONS

Additional books in this series can be found on Nova's website under the Series tab.

Additional e-books in this series can be found on Nova's website under the eBooks tab.

COMPUTER SCIENCE, TECHNOLOGY AND APPLICATIONS

FEDERAL CYBERSECURITY

STRATEGY AND IMPLEMENTATION FOR RESEARCH AND DEVELOPMENT

CORY MEDINA
EDITOR

nova publishers
New York

Library of Congress Cataloging-in-Publication Data

ISBN: 978-1-63485-395-8

Published by Nova Science Publishers, Inc. † New York

CONTENTS

PREFACE

Computers and computer networking provide major benefits to modern society, yet the growing costs of malicious cyber activities and cybersecurity itself diminish these benefits. Advances in cybersecurity are urgently needed to preserve the Internet's growing social and economic benefits by thwarting adversaries and strengthening public trust of cyber systems. On December 18, 2014 the President signed into law the *Cybersecurity Enhancement Act of 2014*. This law requires the National Science and Technology Council (NSTC) and the Networking and Information Technology Research and Development (NITRD) Program to develop and maintain a cybersecurity research and development (R&D) strategic plan (the Plan) using an assessment of risk to guide the overall direction of Federally-funded cybersecurity R&D. This plan satisfies that requirement and establishes the direction for the Federal R&D enterprise in cybersecurity science and technology (S&T) to preserve and expand the Internet's wide-ranging benefits. This book reviews the strategy and implementation for research and development of federal cybersecurity.

In: Federal Cybersecurity
Editor: Cory Medina

ISBN: 978-1-63485-395-8

Chapter 1

FEDERAL CYBERSECURITY RESEARCH AND DEVELOPMENT STRATEGIC PLAN: ENSURING PROSPERITY AND NATIONAL SECURITY*

Networking and Information Technology Research and Development Program

Members of Congress:

I am pleased to transmit with this letter the National Science and Technology Council's (NSTC) *Federal Cybersecurity Research and Development Strategic Plan*. This plan responds to Section 201 of the Cybersecurity Enhancement Act of 2014, which directs the NSTC and the Networking and Information Technology Research and Development (NITRD) Program to develop a strategic plan to guide Federal cybersecurity research and development. It builds on *Trustworthy Cyberspace: Strategic Plan for the Federal Cybersecurity Research and Development Program*, which was released by the NSTC in December 2011.

As a foundation that enables safety and innovation in cyberspace, cybersecurity is of fundamental importance to the economic strength and

* This is an edited, reformatted and augmented version of a document issued by the National Science and Technology Council, February 2016.

national security of the United States. While the United States is increasingly dependent upon cyberspace, cybersecurity has not kept pace with the increase in cyber threats. Advances in cybersecurity science and engineering are urgently needed to preserve the Internet's societal and economic benefits and establish a position of assurance, strength, and trust for cyber systems and professionals. The NSTC's work provides a solid basis for Federal cybersecurity research and development policy. The advances in science and engineering established by this plan will enable fundamental changes in the nature of cyberspace by reversing asymmetric advantages currently enjoyed by adversaries of the United States. The subsequent increase in cybersecurity will enable further innovation, enhancing national security and economic competitiveness. I look forward to working with the Congress and other key partners to realize that goal.

Sincerely,
John P. Holdren
Assistant to the President for Science and Technology Director,
Office of Science and Technology Policy

EXECUTIVE SUMMARY

Computers and computer networking provide major benefits to modern society, yet the growing costs of malicious cyber activities and cybersecurity itself diminish these benefits. Advances in cybersecurity are urgently needed to preserve the Internet's growing social and economic benefits by thwarting adversaries and strengthening public trust of cyber systems.

On December 18, 2014 the President signed into law the *Cybersecurity Enhancement Act of 2014*. This law requires the National Science and Technology Council (NSTC) and the Networking and Information Technology Research and Development (NITRD) Program to develop and maintain a cybersecurity research and development (R&D) strategic plan (the Plan) using an assessment of risk to guide the overall direction of Federally-funded cybersecurity R&D. This plan satisfies that requirement and establishes the direction for the Federal R&D enterprise in cybersecurity science and technology (S&T) to preserve and expand the Internet's wide-ranging benefits.[1]

This strategic plan updates and expands the December 2011 plan, *Trustworthy Cyberspace: Strategic Plan for the Federal Cybersecurity*

Research and Development Program. The 2011 plan defined a set of interrelated breakthrough objectives for Federal agencies that conduct or sponsor R&D in cybersecurity. This Plan incorporates and expands the priorities in the 2011 plan and adds a strong focus on evidence-validated R&D. Evidence of cybersecurity efficacy and efficiency, such as formal proofs and empirical measurements, drives progress in cybersecurity R&D and improves cybersecurity practice.

Four assumptions are the foundation of this plan:

Adversaries. Adversaries will perform malicious cyber activities as long as they perceive that the potential results outweigh the likely effort and possible consequences for themselves.

Defenders. Defenders must thwart malicious cyber activities on increasingly valuable and critical systems with limited resources and despite evolving technologies and threat scenarios.

Users. Users—legitimate individuals and enterprises[2]—will circumvent cybersecurity practices that they perceive as irrelevant, ineffective, inefficient, or overly burdensome.

Technology. As technology cross-connects the physical and cyber worlds, the risks as well as the benefits of the two worlds are interconnected.

The plan defines three research and development goals to provide the science, engineering, mathematics, and technology necessary to improve cybersecurity in light of these assumptions. The science and engineering advances needed are socio-technical in nature, and vary from foundational to applied over a range of time scales:[3]

Near-Term Goal (1-3 years). Achieve S&T advances to counter adversaries' asymmetrical advantages with effective and efficient risk management.

Mid-Term Goal (3-7 Years). Achieve S&T advances to reverse adversaries' asymmetrical advantages, through sustainably secure systems development and operation.

Long-Term Goal (7-15 years). Achieve S&T advances for effective and efficient deterrence of malicious cyber activities via denial of results and likely attribution.

While near-term goals are frequently focused on developing and refining existing science, medium- and long-term goals require both refinement and improvement of existing science, and fundamental research, which has the potential for identifying transformative new approaches to solve problems beyond the current research areas.

To achieve these goals, the Plan focuses on developing S&T to support four defensive elements:

Deter. The ability to efficiently discourage malicious cyber activities by measuring and increasing costs to adversaries carrying out such activities, diminishing the spoils, and increasing risks and uncertainty for potential adversaries.

Protect. The ability of components, systems, users, and critical infrastructure to efficiently resist malicious cyber activities and to ensure confidentiality, integrity, availability, and accountability.

Detect. The ability to efficiently detect, and even anticipate, adversary decisions and activities, given that perfect security is not possible and systems should be assumed to be vulnerable to malicious cyber activities.

Adapt. The ability of defenders, defenses, and infrastructure to dynamically adapt to malicious cyber activities, by efficiently reacting to disruption, recovering from damage, maintaining operations while completing restoration, and adjusting to thwart similar future activity.

After a description of each element and associated research challenges, the Plan identifies research objectives to achieve in each element over the near-, mid-, and long-term. The objectives are not comprehensive but establish a basis to measure progress in implementing the Plan. These elements are applicable throughout cyberspace, although some objectives are most meaningful in particular contexts, such as cloud computing or the Internet of Things (IoT).

The Plan identifies six areas critical to successful cybersecurity R&D: (1) scientific foundations; (2) enhancements in risk management; (3) human aspects; (4) transitioning successful research into pervasive use; (5) workforce development; and (6) enhancing the infrastructure for research.

The Plan closes with five recommendations:

Recommendation 1. Prioritize basic and long-term research in Federal cybersecurity R&D.

Recommendation 2. Lower barriers and strengthen incentives for public and private organizations that would broaden participation in cybersecurity R&D.

Recommendation 3. Assess barriers and identify incentives that could accelerate the transition.

of evidence-validated effective and efficient cybersecurity research results into adopted technologies, especially for emerging technologies and threats.

Recommendation 4. Expand the diversity of expertise in the cybersecurity research community.

Recommendation 5. Expand diversity in the cybersecurity workplace.

Implementing the Plan and these recommendations will create S&T for cybersecurity that effectively and efficiently defends cyberspace and sustains an Internet that is inherently more secure.

1. INTRODUCTION

The modern computing era arrived less than 70 years ago, with the public announcement in 1946 of the Electronic Numerical Integrator And Computer (ENIAC), first used to calculate artillery firing tables. The Internet era was ushered in 23 years later, when the first two ARPANET nodes were established in 1969. In 1993, the Mosaic browser transformed the Internet into an interconnected web of information. Social media's explosion in the following decade made cyberspace an integral component of society's fabric, and accelerated the adoption of smart mobile devices, which provide Internet access from almost every location. Computing and networking underpin critical infrastructure and form the backbone of modern military systems. Today, information technology (IT) is woven into nearly every aspect of modern life, and emerging technologies of the 21st century, such as the IoT and smart cities, promise that cyberspace will continue to offer exceptional benefits to society even as it continues to evolve.[4]

While computing is only 70 years old, cybersecurity is an even younger discipline. Early computing used large systems in data centers that could be protected by guards, guns, and gates. The Internet erased many physical boundaries, but in its early days, it connected only a small cadre of trusted people in academia and government laboratories. Because access was limited to trusted colleagues and resources on the Internet were of relatively limited scope, security was not a significant issue.

In 1988, the Morris Worm brought the Internet to a standstill, and the significance of cybersecurity became clear.[5] While the Internet is far more robust today than it was in 1988, cyber threats have also increased. Today, U.S.

intellectual property is being stolen, critical infrastructure is at risk, commercial and government computer systems are hacked, and consumers are worried about their privacy. As currently deployed, the Internet places both public and private sectors at a major disadvantage with cyber criminals and other malicious adversaries. The more society relies on the benefits of IT, the greater the potential disruption, diversion, and destruction that adversaries can create via malicious cyber activities.[6]

The current trajectories for benefit and risk are unsustainable. One recent report suggests the benefits may be overtaken by cybersecurity costs as early as 2030.[7] Just as brakes enable driving safely at higher speeds, cybersecurity is the foundation that enables economic growth and faster innovation in cyberspace. Advances in cybersecurity are urgently needed to preserve the Internet's societal and economic benefits by establishing a position of assurance, strength, and trust for cyber systems and professionals. Just as Federally-funded research and development (R&D) was essential to the development of ENIAC, ARPANET, and the Internet browser, strategic Federal R&D investments can contribute to these advances in cybersecurity and preserve the benefits it helped create.

On December 18, 2014, the President signed into law the *Cybersecurity Enhancement Act of 2014* (Public Law 113-274). In the second of its five titles, the law requires the NSTC and NITRD Program to develop and maintain, based on an assessment of risk, a cybersecurity R&D strategic plan to guide the overall direction of Federally-funded R&D. This document (the Plan) was developed by interagency subject-matter experts from the NITRD Program and the NSTC, under the leadership of the White House Office of Science and Technology Policy (OSTP). The committee consulted with industry and academia through a Request for Information issued through NITRD and engagements with industry at public conferences to ensure that Federally-funded R&D activities do not duplicate private-sector investments.

This Plan calls for a strong focus on evidence-driven S&T for cybersecurity.[8] Evidence of efficacy and efficiency is needed not only to guide cybersecurity R&D progress, but also to change cybersecurity practice for the better.

This Plan updates and expands the December 2011 strategic plan, *Trustworthy Cyberspace: Strategic Plan for the Federal Cybersecurity Research and Development Program*.[9] That plan defined a set of breakthrough objectives for the agencies of the U.S. Government that conduct or sponsor R&D in cybersecurity. This 2015 plan is more comprehensive, and it incorporates and expands the priorities in the 2011 plan. Both plans demonstrate the maturing Federal approach to cybersecurity R&D as the Nation's demand for effective and efficient cybersecurity grows.

Cybersecurity is a shared responsibility. The private sector, government, and academia all have roles to play in cybersecurity R&D. Government funds long-term, high-risk research and mission-specific R&D. Academia and research institutions perform the majority of this high-risk research. The private sector funds near-term research and transitions successful research into commercial products. This document lays out a research agenda for Federally-funded R&D carried out by government agencies and the U.S. R&D enterprise, informed by interactions with business and academia.

The R&D strategy outlined in this document is shaped by current events, recent Executive Orders (EOs), reports from Presidential advisory committees, and other national policies and initiatives. Specific policy priorities include an emphasis on cybersecurity for critical infrastructure; the incorporation of strong privacy protections into national-security initiatives; information sharing between government and the private sector; and protecting consumers from financial fraud.

The President recognized the dangers in U.S. technology dependence and identified cybersecurity for the Nation's critical infrastructure as an urgent priority in 2013, issuing EO 13636, Improving Critical Infrastructure Cybersecurity[10], and Presidential Policy Directive (PPD) 21, Critical Infrastructure Security and Resilience.[11] Cybersecurity is also featured in the National Preparedness Goal[12] and highlighted in PPD 8 National Preparedness, which identified five mission areas for strengthening security and resilience against the threats and hazards that pose the greatest risk to the Nation.[13] (For additional information on the relationship of this Plan with PPD-8, see Appendix C.)

In 2013, the President's Council of Advisors on Science and Technology (PCAST) issued the report *Immediate Opportunities for Improving Cybersecurity*. One of the key findings in that report reflects the fragile nature of the IT base:

> Future architectures will need to start with the premise that each part of a system must be designed to operate in a hostile environment. Research is needed to foster systems with dynamic, real-time defenses to complement traditional hardening approaches, such as firewalls and virus scanners.[14,15]

In its 2015 Review of the NITRD program, PCAST further indicated the fragile nature of IT when it recommended broad foundational research and more applied mission-appropriate investigations, on:

> ...methods to facilitate end-to-end construction of trustworthy systems, particularly for emerging application domains, and on ways to anticipate and defend against attacks, engaging not only computer science but also other engineering disciplines and behavioral and social science.[16]

Another theme is cybersecurity's role as an enabler of privacy. Disclosures of classified intelligence activities and exfiltration of personal information from government and corporate systems created a broad national discussion of privacy and confidentiality in the context of national security and cybersecurity. The January 2013 PCAST report on the NITRD Program cited privacy and protected disclosure as a cross-cutting theme, "...one that is important for every agency and mission, as huge amounts of diverse information about individuals become available in online electronic form." [17]

Another of the key findings from the 2013 PCAST cybersecurity report addressed information sharing:

> To improve the capacity to respond in real time, cyber threat data need to be shared more extensively among private-sector entities and—in appropriate circumstances and with publicly understood interfaces—between private-sector entities and Government.[18]

The importance of information sharing for critical infrastructure was also highlighted in PPD-21, and the Administration has encouraged legislative initiatives to address information sharing in other sectors.

Authentication is a recurring theme in recent policy initiatives. The 2011 *National Strategy for Trusted Identities in Cyberspace* (NSTIC) highlighted the importance of privacy,[19] security, and ease-of-use of authentication for sensitive online transactions, and Federal Information Processing Standard 201-2 established common authentication standards for Federal employees.[20] In 2013, EO 13681, Improving the Security of Consumer Financial Transactions, identified strong authentication as a foundational tool for consumer protection.[21] Policy initiatives involving cyber-physical systems, such as the National Security Telecommunications Advisory Committee (NSTAC) November 2014 report *NSTAC Report to the President on the*

Internet of Things,[22] have demonstrated an additional need for more secure authentication of network devices.

This strategic plan is inspired by the context of the events and policy statements described above. The strategic R&D portfolio it lays out will increase the breadth and robustness of cybersecurity measures for IT, and will support the policy priorities highlighted above. The framework and priorities set forth in this Plan must continue to evolve as understanding of threats, challenges, and solutions improves and as new policies are implemented.

The remainder of this document presents the core parts of the Plan, organized in five sections. The first section, Strategic Framing, provides a vision statement, the articulation of challenges, the cybersecurity elements this Plan seeks to establish, and a set of critical dependencies. The next section, Defensive Elements, expands upon the R&D challenges for each defensive element in turn, along with its respective near-, mid-, and long-term objectives. The third section, Emerging Technologies and Applications, relates these elements to emerging technology areas, such as IOT, and provides examples of technology-specific research priorities. The fourth section, Critical Dependencies, details challenges and objectives for the six cross-cutting issues. The fifth section, Implementation of the Plan, outlines the roles and responsibilities of Federal agencies, the private sector, universities, and other research organizations. This section of the Plan also identifies coordination mechanisms within government and with the private sector. The Plan closes with recommendations, as requested in the *Cybersecurity Enhancement Act of 2014*.

2. STRATEGIC FRAMING

This strategic plan for cybersecurity R&D is based on an analysis of the current and future risk environment, and opportunities for cybersecurity R&D to best address those risks. The strategy focuses on thwarting malicious cyber activities by developing S&T to support four defensive elements—Deter, Protect, Detect, and Adapt—using socio-technical approaches. This strategy is driven by evidence-based evaluations and measurements of the efficacy and efficiency of cybersecurity S&T solutions. They are effective if they achieve the desired security result; they are efficient when the measured units-of-benefit is greater than the minimized units-of-cost. These criteria guide the search for ever-improving solutions from evolutionary and game-changing innovations.

This section lays out an analytic framing based on existing and emerging cybersecurity risks, underlying assumptions, and the primary S&T challenges to define the Plan's vision and goals. The framing then defines the defensive elements and areas of critical dependencies essential to reaching the desired outcome of inherently more secure cyber systems.

Risks

This Plan considers the cybersecurity threats that exist today and those that are likely to emerge in the next 10 years. Current information systems and infrastructure are used in increasingly vital tasks, such as controlling critical infrastructure, but are widely known to possess vulnerabilities that are easy to discover and difficult to correct. Remedies are often expensive to implement, especially at scale. New systems and infrastructure are created with the same weak development processes, introducing the next generation of vulnerabilities. Meanwhile, the Internet and cyberspace in general continue to grow in value, complexity, diversity, and scale, and even traditional companies are becoming IT-intensive. The technical vulnerabilities of cyberspace are exacerbated by inherent and easy-to-exploit human weaknesses that result in on-line and off-line social-engineering manipulations, such as phishing. The many security mechanisms and procedures immediately available are often unreliable or require significant resources to implement. Human resources are constrained by a growing gap in cybersecurity workforce size, diversity, capabilities, and agility.

Adversaries include state actors and non-state actors; their skills and capacities cover a wide range, from amateurish hacks using simple tools to highly sophisticated operators with artisanal tradecraft. Their motivations vary widely, as do the levels of resources they have to pursue their objectives. Given the continued preponderance of easy targets, these adversaries seize opportunities for easy gains. They will continue malicious cyber activities to exploit vulnerable systems, and their sophistication will continue to grow.

Given these risks, this Plan makes four key assumptions:

Adversaries. Adversaries will perform malicious cyber activities as long as they perceive that the potential results outweigh the likely effort and possible consequences for themselves.

Defenders. Defenders must thwart malicious cyber activities on increasingly valuable and critical systems with limited resources and despite evolving technologies and threat scenarios.

Users. Users—legitimate individuals and enterprises—will circumvent cybersecurity practices that they perceive as irrelevant, ineffective, inefficient, or overly burdensome.

Technology. As technology cross-connects the physical and cyber worlds, the risks as well as the benefits of the two worlds are interconnected.

Challenges

The fundamental research challenge is to make cybersecurity less onerous while providing more-effective defenses. The Plan seeks to improve existing technologies and practices to foster secure systems, while at the same time discovering and applying innovations that offer greater ease of use, effectiveness, and scalability that require less cost, human capital investment, and effort to deploy and operate. In this way, users will reap the benefits of IT, improve productivity, and accelerate innovation with fewer risks to themselves and their organizations.

Realization of the Plan requires evidence of cybersecurity efficacy and efficiency; the R&D community needs to establish and achieve measurable cybersecurity objectives. Requiring evidence of efficacy and efficiency is not the same as creating quantitative measures of cybersecurity. Evidence-based approaches require significant work to answer questions such as what can be measured, what data can be collected, and even what is the nature of evaluation in the cybersecurity context. An evidence-based approach for cybersecurity is crucial to identify truly game-changing innovations and is the basis for meaningful feedback loops in evolutionary approaches. The critical need for such evidence applies to all R&D for socio-technical solutions in cybersecurity.

Though it is not the focus of this Plan, it is important for cybersecurity researchers to consider and document the privacy impacts of new cybersecurity technologies and mechanisms to ensure that privacy risks are identified and mitigated at the beginning of and throughout the life cycle of any new cyber mechanism. Privacy cannot exist without the foundation of cybersecurity's confidentiality, access control, and authentication mechanisms, but carelessly implemented cybersecurity controls can negatively impact privacy. A privacy and confidentiality R&D strategy is being developed for release in 2016.

Similarly, policies designed to enforce cybersecurity may be at odds with operating safety-critical systems that must provide continuous operation, such as air-traffic control, flight-control systems, refineries, power grids, and medical devices. In many situations, integrity and availability are the dominant properties of interest. In a degraded system (due to, say, random faults), one may choose to prioritize availability over other considerations. A security-focused policy might prioritize confidentiality or integrity above availability. A systems development framework must be equipped to handle the possible tradeoffs between security and safety considerations. As cyber-physical systems with distributed control authority become prevalent, the difficulty of managing these tradeoffs will increase. This underscores the need for a sophisticated Federal IT cadre of cybersecurity personnel that can continuously evaluate and adapt to the evolving cyber threat landscape, based on evidence, as well as intelligence on the tactics, techniques, and procedures of adversaries.

Vision

If this Plan is successful, the cybersecurity research, development, and operations community will quickly design, develop, deploy, and operate effective new cybersecurity technologies and services, while cybersecurity tasks for users will be few and easy to accomplish. In this environment, many adversaries will be deterred from launching malicious cyber activities, and those that choose to proceed will fail or fail to impact the user or organization's mission.

With the challenge of making cybersecurity less obtrusive and more effective, it is important to remember that when these are lacking, adversaries will have advantages that they will exploit. For cyber adversaries, identifying vulnerabilities and developing ways to exploit them is faster than the lifecycle of developing and deploying fixes for those vulnerabilities, allowing them to stay well ahead of those who protect the systems. This is a classic example of an asymmetric advantage: today it takes far more effort, resources, and time to defend cyber systems than the effort, resources, and time it takes the adversaries to carry out malicious activities. This asymmetry must be reversed.

Integral to this vision for cybersecurity R&D is ensuring that new technologies and applications are put into practice in a timely and efficient way, in order for security measures to keep pace with the emerging tactics, techniques, and procedures employed by adversaries. As part of the Plan's vision to fund research through the full R&D lifecycle—research, development, testing, evaluation, and transition—it aims to identify technologies with a high probability of success that address gaps in critical systems, and to facilitate rapid transfer of research results to potential users, including the dissemination of best practices and outreach activities. Understanding the role of humans as defenders, users, and adversaries is an important (and often underappreciated) aspect of cybersecurity, especially in large IT-intensive enterprises and ecosystems. The Plan envisions partnerships between the research community, the Federal government, industry, and end users, in order to bridge the gap between research and eventual use, and to avoid unnecessarily duplicative public-sector efforts.

Along with an investment in technology solutions, the Plan highlights the importance of investments in the cyber workforce. Achieving the vision will require a diverse workforce of cyber professionals who can design, develop, and implement suitable cybersecurity measures, as well as assessing and managing risk.

Goals

The plan defines three research and development goals to provide the science, engineering, mathematics, and technology necessary to improve cybersecurity in light of these assumptions.[23] The science and engineering advances needed are socio-technical in nature, and can range from foundational to applied, over a range of time scales. The near-term goal provides S&T advances for individual organizations. The mid-term goal applies across organizations, but does not encompass the entire cyber ecosystem. The long-term goal applies to the complete cyber ecosystem.

Near-Term Goal (1-3 years). Achieve S&T advances to counter adversaries' asymmetrical advantages with effective and efficient risk management.

To accomplish this, organizations need a sound understanding of the range of vulnerabilities and threats in cyberspace. This involves evidence-based risk management, which is the process of identifying, assessing, and responding to risk, including the development of effective and measurable controls. Organizations must have access to evidence of the efficacy and efficiency for these controls and consider the human aspects with respect to users, developers, operators, defenders, and adversaries. Achieving this goal will enhance understanding of effective measures against malicious cyber activities and thereby lower their likelihood and overall cybersecurity risks.

Mid-Term Goal (3-7 Years). Achieve S&T advances to reverse adversaries' asymmetrical advantages, through sustainably secure systems development and operation.

This goal is two-pronged: first, the design and implementation of software, firmware, and hardware that are highly resistant to malicious cyber activities (e.g., software defects, which are common, give rise to many vulnerabilities); and second, the development of effective, measurable technical and non-technical security controls that consider human behavior as well as economic drivers associated with cyberspace (e.g., too often system breaches are due to accidental actions by unwitting users). Organizations must improve the efficacy and efficiency of their defenses by several orders of magnitude without placing undue burden on users, making malicious cyber activities more difficult, and reducing the rewards of such activities.

Long-Term Goal (7-15 years). Achieve S&T advances for effective and efficient deterrence of malicious cyber activities via denial of results and likely attribution.

Deterrence is the ability to discourage malicious cyber activities by increasing costs, lowering gains, and increasing risks for adversaries. The mid-term goal provides the foundation for increasing adversary effort required for malicious cyber activities and reducing the gains from those activities. Measuring the effort required and the likely results for malicious activities is critical to understanding the degree to which denial effectively deters such activities.

Increasing risks to adversaries requires accurate attribution, which can be difficult, as the origins of individual actions in cyberspace are easy to disguise and verifiable evidence of malicious cyber activity is not always attainable in a timely manner. A high-confidence forensic capacity that identifies the perpetrator within an actionable timeframe, without compromising free speech or anonymity, will increase the likelihood of their discovery and the negative consequences that they will suffer and ideally preemptively cause them to abandon their malicious activities.

Desired Defensive Elements

Given the above goals, the Plan focuses on developing S&T to support four defensive elements:

Deter. The ability to efficiently discourage malicious cyber activities by: measuring and increasing costs to adversaries carrying out such activities; diminishing the spoils; and increasing risks and uncertainty for potential adversaries.

Protect. The ability of components, systems, users, and critical infrastructure to efficiently resist malicious cyber activities, and to ensure confidentiality, integrity, availability, and accountability.

Detect. The ability to efficiently detect, and even anticipate adversary decisions and activities, given that perfect security is not possible and systems should be assumed to be vulnerable to malicious cyber activities.

Adapt. The ability of defenders, defenses, and infrastructure to dynamically adapt to malicious cyber activities by efficiently reacting to disruption, recovering from damage, maintaining operations while completing restoration, and adjusting to thwart similar future activity.

These four elements are similar but not identical to the five core functions in the National Institute of Standards and Technology's (NIST) *Framework for Improving Critical Infrastructure Cybersecurity*.[24] This plan is intended to guide cybersecurity R&D and is therefore broader in scope, while the five NIST core functions are for operational cybersecurity risk management. This Plan discusses risk management as a critical dependency. (Appendix B expands on the relationship between this Plan's four defensive elements and the NIST framework's Core Functions.)

Figure 1 shows how these four defensive elements thwart malicious cyber activities and the value of continuous outcome-driven improvements in efficacy and efficiency.

Critical Dependencies

Advancements in the following six areas are critical to developing the S&T for the four elements:

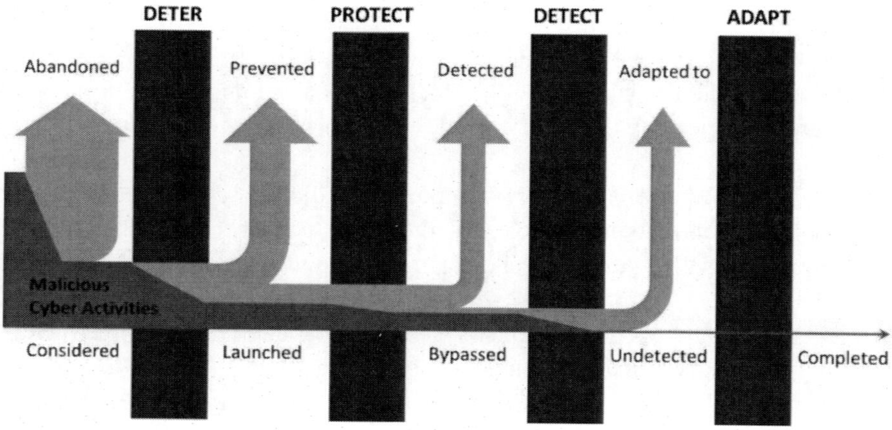

Figure 1. Continuously strengthening defensive elements improves success in thwarting malicious cyber activities.

Scientific foundation. The Federal Government should support research that establishes the theoretical, empirical, computational, and data mining foundation needed to address future threats. A strong, rigorous scientific foundation for cybersecurity identifies methods of measurement, testable models, and formal frameworks, as well as forecasting techniques that express the essential security dynamics of cyber systems and processes. Such foundational understanding is the primary basis for developing effective defensive cyber technologies and practices.

*Risk management***.** Cybersecurity decisions in an organization should be based on a shared assessment of the organization's assets, vulnerabilities, and potential threats, so that security investments can be risk-informed. This must be achieved despite the incomplete knowledge the organization has of its assets, vulnerabilities, exposures, and potential threats. An effective risk management approach requires an ability to assess the likelihood of malicious cyber activity and its possible consequences, and correctly quantify costs resulting from successful exploitation and risk mitigation. Timely, risk-relevant threat intelligence information sharing can improve organizations' abilities to assess and manage risks.

*Human aspects***.** Researchers are capable of developing innovative technical solutions for protecting cyber systems, but those solutions will fail if they do not recognize how users, defenders, adversaries, and institutions interact with technology. Beyond helping to address the challenges of human-system interactions, collaborative engagement of social scientists in cybersecurity research can increase understanding of the social, behavioral, and economic aspects of cybersecurity and how to improve collective risk governance.

Transition to practice. A well-articulated, coordinated process that transitions the fruits of research into practice is essential to ensure high-impact Federal cybersecurity R&D. The research community, which focuses on developing and demonstrating novel and innovative technologies, and the operational community, which needs to integrate solutions into existing industry products and services, are not always aligned. An effective technology transfer program must be an integral part of any R&D strategy and rely on sustained and significant public-private participation.

Cybersecurity workforce. Developing a cybersecurity workforce that can meet the demands described in this Plan remains a key challenge. People are an essential component of cyber systems, and can contribute to security (or insecurity) in a variety of ways. The success or failure of this Plan depends largely upon expanding and retaining a sufficient number of diverse and highly-skilled cybersecurity researchers, product developers, and cybersecurity professionals. In addition, R&D can provide tools to make the cyber workforce more productive—a force multiplier.

Research infrastructure. Sound science in cybersecurity research must have a basis in controlled and well-executed experiments with operational relevance and realism. That requires tools and test environments that provide access to datasets at the right scale and fidelity, ensure integrity of the experimental process, and support a broad range of interactions, analysis, and validation methods. The Federal Government should encourage the sharing of high-fidelity data sets for research and provide protections to those organizations that voluntarily share their sensitive data with researchers. Investments in research infrastructure should support the needs not only of computer scientists and engineers, but also of other sectors with cybersecurity research challenges, such as critical infrastructure in energy, transportation, and healthcare.

Desired Outcome

The value created by computing and networks will continue to be subverted by those seeking illicit gains. IT systems should be assumed to be vulnerable to malicious cyber activities, and perfect security is not possible. Therefore, effective deterrence must raise the cost of malicious cyber activities, lower their gains, and convince adversaries that such activities can be attributed. Having systems succeed in the face of malicious cyber activity is also key, so that they can continue to deliver critical services even when compromised. This strategy will be successful when cybersecurity solutions and technologies provide orders-of-magnitude improvements in effectiveness and efficiency over current approaches. This will eliminate the advantages that adversaries currently have, especially the ability to reuse the same malicious methods across many systems because system defenders are not mitigating vulnerabilities as quickly as the adversary discovers and exploits them. In addition, adversaries leverage current market dynamics where cost and time-to-market are valued more than attention to security. The strategic plan's cybersecurity framing of Deter, Protect, Detect, and Adapt addresses the range of cybersecurity needs, and by doing so, provides a structure for coordinating research and focusing on shared goals. Achieving these outcomes will help lead to a world where the Internet and cyber systems in general are inherently more secure.

3. Defensive Elements

This section describes each of the elements in greater detail, providing a summary of the current state of the art, describing possible impediments, and identifying promising research avenues for each.

Each defensive element also has selected near-term, mid-term, and long-term research objectives. The stated objectives highlight some promising research areas with their expected impact and provide a basis for measuring overall progress in the implementation of this plan. They do not address all areas of need and should not be considered comprehensive. As with the overall goals specified in the preceding section, the target completion of near-term objectives is for 1-3 years from this Plan's publication, mid-term objectives for 3-7 years from publication, and long-term objectives for 7-15 years from publication.

3.1. Deter

The most effective way to secure a system, network, or enterprise from cyber threats is deterrence, the ability to increase the adversary's level of effort required to achieve their objectives and the possible negative consequences of their actions. If adversaries judge that the likely costs of malicious activities, including the risk of prosecution or sanctions, are greater than the expected results, they are more likely to be deterred from attempting the activity. There are a variety of actions that system and network owners, law enforcement, and government agencies can take to enhance deterrence. Deterrence first requires effective and multi-pronged defenses in order to increase the resources required by an adversary. Currently, malicious activities that cause significant impact can be executed for just thousands or tens of thousands of dollars. Proven adversary techniques remain disappointingly effective, and new techniques are quickly packaged into malicious tools requiring only modest technical skill. A successful cyber defense has many facets, ranging from the appropriate technological solutions (e.g., designing secure software, hardware, and operating systems) to network protocols and access controls to human factors, such as instructing users to use safe data handling methods. Cyber defense can be enhanced with more accurate threat models.

Attribution can also dissuade potential offenders. However, identifying the origins of individual malicious actions in cyberspace can be difficult, as the actors are often in a different jurisdiction than the systems they attempt to breach and operate through proxies and other anonymizing procedures. If they successfully breach security, they are often able to delete logs to cover their tracks.

Effective deterrence also relies on the other elements reviewed below—Protect, Detect, and Adapt. Protection means to successfully avoid or ward off malicious cyber activities and prevent damage or disruption of systems, or loss of vital information or even threats to national security. For example, malicious activities are more difficult if software has fewer exploitable vulnerabilities, and hardware and firmware are more tamper resistant. Robust situational awareness, with strong indications and warning abilities, limits the time a successful adversary remains in the system and inhibit lateral movement within the enterprise. Cyber forensics can provide many details about adversaries' methods and identity, exposing adversaries to law enforcement and prosecution. Finally, adapting with resilience means that malicious activities result in minimal disruption of operations and minimal financial or security losses. Adaptive strategies include sharing information about adversaries' techniques and corresponding mitigations quickly with other defenders; temporarily isolating critical systems and networks in encrypted enclaves; or requiring that using (stolen) personal data requires a second authentication step that is difficult to spoof. Protection, detection, and adaptation all contribute to deterrence by increasing the costs and decreasing the results of malicious activities.

Challenges

Malicious cyber activities occur in the virtual domain, but governments impose costs in the "real world." Financial sanctions may be applied to people, companies, and state entities, not to email addresses or computer accounts. While the ability to attribute malicious activity to a specific actor through long-term analysis has improved dramatically in recent years, allowing for such actors to be held responsible for their actions, high-confidence attribution in real-time remains challenging. Another challenge is developing forensic techniques robust enough to preserve evidence suitable for use in legal proceedings, while also bolstering immediate detection and cyber analytical abilities.

The key technical challenge for this aspect of deterrence is quantifying the resources an adversary would require to successfully breach or evade cybersecurity controls or detection. Threat modeling is one way to accomplish this.

To meet these challenges, new technologies are needed to measure and verify the ability of the enterprise to thwart adversary efforts, and to ensure that law enforcement, government agencies, and system and network owners can successfully attribute malicious activities to their source. Examples of these technologies are:

Measurement of adversary level of effort, results, and risks. Measurement provides the feedback essential to improving defenses and to assessing the overall ability to thwart malicious cyber activities. Adversary level of effort could be measured in dollars (if an exploit can be purchased on the black market, contracted out, or fashioned from the salaries of in-house staff), in person-hours of effort, electrical power, or computing resources (e.g., petaflops and terabytes). Where adversaries are deterred because the level of effort is too high relative to the available capacities, the potential gains, or the risks of consequences from malicious activities, they are likely to consider and pursue alternative forms of action. Thus, a corollary to measuring adversary level of effort would be assessing and costing possible alternative actions so as to better anticipate them.

Effective and timely attribution. Accurate attribution of malicious cyber activities to their sources opens up a broad range of response options, such as sanctions, prosecution, and even military actions in appropriately limited circumstances.

Robust investigative tools. Effective investigative tools for law enforcement create the basis for evidence required for successful prosecution of cyber adversaries. These tools must be sufficiently robust to stand up as evidence in court. Alternatively, law enforcement must have valid options to demonstrate the chain of custody without revealing sources or methods.

Information sharing for attribution. Effective mechanisms for sharing information to support efficient attribution are needed to support investigations that cross international or domestic law enforcement jurisdictions.

R&D Objectives

Near-term:

- Establish quantifiable metrics of adversary level of effort needed to overcome specific cybersecurity defenses, as well as assess the viability and cost of alternative courses of action to achieve the same or similar objectives.
- Determine what probability of attribution and criminal or economic sanctions would be necessary to deter various types of malicious cyber activities and adversaries.

Mid-term:

- Automatically extract information about malicious cyber activities to document, verify, and share among law enforcement agencies and other partners to support attribution in near-real time.

Long-term:

- Accurately and efficiently attribute malicious cyber activities to specific actors, companies, or nation states, with sufficient precision to support imposition of costs or economic sanctions and sufficient probability to deter malicious activities.

3.2. Protect

The second defensive element, Protect, focuses on creating systems and networks that are highly resistant to malicious cyber activities through assurance-based engineering practices, which will simultaneously protect a system and supply the verifiable evidence needed to support its assurance case.

Today, virtually every computing system is vulnerable to some form of malicious cyber activity. While continuous improvements in system security are being made, progress is often ad hoc and difficult to measure. Many products have been shipped with large numbers of vulnerabilities,[25] and security controls can be circumvented in practice (e.g., by social engineering).[26] As a result, adversaries find the level of effort required to penetrate systems and networks acceptable in many cases.

Commercial software products that make up a typical computer or mobile device include millions of lines of code, many of which are carried over into successive generations of software through open-source repositories. These products are estimated to include one software defect for every thousand lines of code.[27] Some of these defects create security vulnerabilities, resulting in a cyber ecosystem that is difficult to defend, in spite of efforts to deploy strong security controls and protocols. The security of web servers and many other products are often undermined by small but subtle software coding errors, as illustrated by the "Heartbleed" vulnerability.[28]

Vulnerabilities in hardware design appear to be less common than in software, primarily because of structured design techniques, but they can be more serious, potentially allowing adversaries to bypass protections.

Hardware and firmware may have vulnerabilities such as timing errors, surreptitiously added logic, or information leaks. Achieving effective hardware and firmware protection will require advances similar to those required for software. Today, the exploitation of software vulnerabilities generally precedes malicious cyber activities on hardware or firmware (e.g., adversaries gain system or application level access, then leverage that to penetrate the hardware and maintain a persistent presence). Reductions in software vulnerability, without corresponding reductions in the number of vulnerabilities in hardware and firmware, will only shift adversaries' focus.[29]

Given a system with a manageable number of security vulnerabilities, achieving high resistance to malicious cyber activities will require effective and efficient security controls and protocols. Cryptographic algorithms, for example, offer quantifiable levels of resistance to specific malicious activities, when implemented correctly. This known level of resistance allows designers to select the appropriate algorithm for a particular system or application.

Many current security controls offer limited or undocumented efficacy, place a burdensome workload on administrators and authorized users, or rely on unrealistic assumptions about the environment or user behavior. All too often, security controls are implemented without proof of effectiveness and imposed on an unwilling user community in an environment that differs radically from the developer's expectations. Current best practices rely on firewalls and virtual private networks to establish a virtual castle, but users' susceptibility to phishing provides adversaries with an alternative entry point.[30] Multi-factor authentication increases security by increasing attack complexity, but users have largely rejected this effective approach to authentication as too cumbersome, particularly when faced with different authentication tokens on different systems.[31]

Challenges

Strengthening protection requires increasing assurance that the products people develop and deploy are highly resistant to malicious cyber activities, because they include very few vulnerabilities and offer effective and efficient security controls to enforce security policies.

Limiting Vulnerabilities

Limiting the number of vulnerabilities in products is a challenge, because vulnerabilities can be introduced at any stage of the product lifecycle. There are five essential aspects needed to produce software, hardware, or firmware with fewer defects that present security vulnerabilities: (1) designing with security in mind; (2) using tools and techniques that produce code with fewer vulnerabilities; (3) testing to identify remaining vulnerabilities; (4) correcting flaws in deployed products; and (5) ensuring that the deployed product is genuine and does not include unwanted functionality.

Design for security. In many cases, security vulnerabilities are present from the start. To avoid systemic security vulnerabilities, system architects must begin with accurate threat models, a well-defined deployment environment, and a robust understanding of the intended application. On this foundation, the architect must apply well-established security principles (e.g., minimizing the privileges required for a system action) and reliable mechanisms (e.g., cryptography, fine-grained access control) to ensure that all components and processes maintain confidentiality, integrity, and availability as appropriate for the application. Ideally, the architect's designs would be implemented without flaws that make them vulnerable, but it is not practical to construct systems that are entirely free of security flaws. Architects must assume that the system will include faulty or malicious components and design the system to maintain security properties during the course of computation.

Achieving this vision will require advances in research:

- Architectural assurance tools for precise threat modeling and definition of complex deployment environments, such as Bring Your Own Device (BYOD) policies, cloud computing, and IoT.
- Policy design tools that can derive and verify fine-grained implementation policies for least privilege (e.g., detailed access controls for each file or resource) from human-readable mission policies and objectives. Fine-grained least privilege can substantially reduce what an adversary can accomplish after an exploit.
- Broadly applicable techniques for evidence-based assessment of efficacy and efficiency for the mechanisms currently available to enforce these principles. Where efficacy and efficiency of existing mechanisms is lacking, new techniques for enforcing security principles will be needed. (Some specific examples appear below under the subheading, Enforcing Security Principles.)
- Verified computation techniques that seek to attain secure, authenticated computation using untrusted components. Published results have established the theoretical feasibility of such approaches, but much remains to be done to bring such techniques into practical use.
- Design tools for effective cyber hygiene, in order to improve detection and make it harder for adversaries to hide or persist.

Build secure. Implementation errors can undermine the security of well-designed components. Although common vulnerabilities such as buffer overflows and memory leaks are well understood by most developers, they are difficult to completely eliminate in practice. Existing tools and practices that prevent developers from creating specific security vulnerabilities, or at least make it easier to identify and correct them, are imperfect and inefficient. To reduce the number of common vulnerabilities in products, tools and practices for software and hardware development are needed that have significantly lower impact on developer productivity and operational system performance.

Formal methods for analyzing software during the development phase would enable implementers to identify less obvious vulnerabilities and would also facilitate detecting vulnerabilities in existing software. Formal methods include a broad array of automated reasoning tools, such as constraint solvers and static program analyses. The applicability of these techniques is currently limited to modest programs with tens-of-thousands of lines of code. Improvements in efficacy and efficiency may make it possible to apply formal methods to systems of practical complexity, resulting in new software systems with fewer vulnerabilities.

Verify security. Even when products are designed for security and robustly built, implementation errors will creep in during system development. In addition to functional testing, components should be subjected to rigorous security analysis throughout the development process before deployment. Static analysis tools evaluate source code or executable computer binaries to identify security vulnerabilities. Fuzzing tools present software with unexpected inputs to identify buffer overflows, system crashes, and other exceptions that can lead to denial of service or system vulnerabilities. Because adversaries also use these tools to find zero-day vulnerabilities (software vulnerabilities that are unknown to the vendor), rigorous application of these tools prevent malicious cyber activities by identifying and eliminating vulnerabilities before a product goes to market.

Maintain security. Inevitably, even software that is well-designed, implemented by knowledgeable developers with good tools, and subjected to comprehensive security testing will still have defects. When errors are identified, the software must be updated. The mechanisms used to update software can unintentionally introduce vulnerabilities instead of eliminating them. A secure mechanism for updating software or firmware is an essential aspect for securing products throughout their lifecycle.

Verify authenticity. The four aspects listed above offer the potential to dramatically reduce the number of vulnerabilities in hardware and software, but only if users deploy authentic, unaltered products. Objective measures for supply-chain assurance are needed to increase an organization's ability to confirm that products are genuine, have not been modified, and do not include additional unwanted functionality. Design and manufacture of computing and communications hardware and software are done globally, and the supply chains are made up of diverse interactions among suppliers, integrators, and servicers. The complexity of this supply chain creates opportunities for adversaries to insert counterfeits, tamper with products, and introduce malicious software and hardware. These malicious cyber activities are difficult to detect, and are believed to provide adversaries with more persistent access than malware.

Current best practices for supply-chain management are focused on subjective attributes (e.g., country of origin), despite uncertain efficacy. Research into objective measures for supply-chain assurance (e.g., cryptology-based markers) is needed to better identify genuine products or those that have not been modified and do not include unwanted functionality. In addition, new hardware mechanisms are needed to ensure both hardware and software authenticity. Hardware, firmware, and software offer different challenges for supply-chain assurance, and unlike development assurance, techniques may not apply across multiple sectors.

Enforcing Security Principles

As noted above, under Design for Security, new techniques for enforcing security principles are needed where efficacy and efficiency is lacking in current mechanisms. Several important examples are listed below:

Authenticate users and systems. User authentication is a traditional building block for enforcement of security policy, but deployment of strong multi-factor authentication systems continues to present challenges. Increasing the efficiency of multi-factor authentication to meet user expectations is a key research priority. The proliferation of IoT and autonomous systems increases the need for strong and efficient authentication of devices.

Access controls. Access controls build upon authentication to support the implementation of security policies and authorizations. Systems often rely on coarse grained access control even though more robust mechanisms (e.g., role-based access control) are available. To accurately enforce security policies, improvements in efficiency are needed for system administrators. In particular, new lightweight hardware security mechanisms to enforce integrity and separation would establish a practical foundation for access control.

Cryptographic mechanisms to data. When other protection mechanisms fail and an adversary gains access to IT systems, or when data are transmitted across networks where eavesdropping is possible, cryptographic methods deny access to plaintext and ensure that adversary modifications do not escape notice. Effective cryptographic mechanisms exist for many applications, but they may not work in constrained environments, such as extremely lightweight systems used in IoT. Researchers can also create more effective cryptographic methods in niche applications. While decryption of data is currently required to perform system operations or modifications, thus creating opportunities for a patient adversary, more efficient techniques that operate directly on encrypted data would offer greater security and privacy. The security offered by common cryptographic algorithms could be weakened or defeated entirely by the advent of quantum computing. Although the timeframe for practical deployment of quantum computing remains unclear, protecting highly sensitive information from such systems will require the development of efficient and effective quantum-resistant algorithms.

Mitigate vulnerabilities. Current systems include many legacy components with undiscovered and unmitigated vulnerabilities, and this may be the case for some time. Game-changing technologies are needed to neutralize malicious cyber activities on legacy systems. Data analytics, the science of examining raw data in order to draw conclusions about that data, offers new opportunities to capitalize on security data and identify malicious activities in the absence of established signatures.

R&D Objectives Near-term:

- Develop secure update mechanisms that support the full range of product formats (i.e., proprietary and open source), applications (e.g., enterprise services and IoT), and lifecycles.
- Develop tools and techniques for evidence-based assessment to determine the efficacy and efficiency of widely-available protection technologies.
- Make cryptographic tools and techniques available for constrained environments (e.g., lightweight cryptography), privacy-preserving applications (e.g., private databases), and longterm confidentiality (e.g., quantum-resistant cryptography).

Mid-Term:

- Create tools for static and dynamic analysis that reduce vulnerabilities in traditionally developed code bases to one defect per ten thousand lines of code (reducing the number of vulnerabilities in new and legacy code bases by a factor of ten).
- Develop automated tools and techniques to derive fine grained security policies implementing least privilege from high-level, mission-oriented policy.
- Develop tools and techniques to verify authenticity and provenance of software and firmware with 98 percent accuracy.

Long-term:

- Create tool chains that support development of software with one defect per hundred thousand lines of code with a relative efficiency metric of 90 percent for productivity and system performance (i.e., systems with 1 percent of the defects in current systems that take no more than 10 percent longer to implement and run up to 10 percent slower than unprotected systems).
- Enhance efficacy and efficiency of security controls, as demonstrated by evidence-based assessment tools and techniques, by two orders of magnitude over 10 years.
- Demonstrate repeatable methodologies for correct computation.

3.3. Detect

Deterrence and protection mechanisms aim to reduce the number of malicious cyber activities attempted and the percentage of those malicious activities that have any significant impact. As long as IT systems store or transmit data of value or manage critical cyber-physical systems of strategic value, malicious cyber activities will continue to be launched, and some number of those activities will warrant detection.

Detection seeks to ensure that system and network owners and users have situational awareness and understanding of ongoing (authorized and malicious) activities, and move towards largely automated detection and warning abilities.

Large-scale cyber situational awareness and understanding remain a challenge today. According to the 2015 Mandiant data breach report, the median time that adversaries were present on a victim network before they were discovered was approximately 6 months.[32] The actual situation is worse, because this does not include breaches that were never detected. Organizations still have difficulty detecting breaches. In 2014, only 31 percent of the organizations that responded to Mandiant had discovered the intrusion themselves; the remainder learned of the intrusion from an external source.

State-of-the-art approaches to cyber defense typically focus on the detection of known cyber events and related artifacts in the later phases of malicious activity; analysis is often ex-post in order to investigate and discover new indicators from the earlier phases. As malicious cyber activities have increased and methods have evolved over the years, established approaches (e.g., signature-based detection, anomaly detection) have not adequately enabled cybersecurity practitioners to stay ahead of these threats.

The gap between aspirations for detection and the current state of detection is striking. It is clear that defenders are not detecting malicious cyber activities at the earliest possible time. It seems very likely that many completed and ongoing malicious activities are never detected; some are probably completed and the tracks are cleaned up, while others likely continue to this day.

Challenges

Enterprise systems and networks are highly complex, with a variety of users in disparate and often dynamic roles. In theory, continuous monitoring of users and timely review of audit logs allow a system owner or operator to discern the presence of current users, how they are connected, and what they are doing. In practice, system owners and operators will require improvements in fidelity and efficiency to make full use of these tools. Adding to the challenge is the volume of information that must be understood in real time. Establishing and maintaining situational awareness and understanding is a challenge, but is an essential first step towards detecting malicious cyber activities.

While researchers envision a future where most detection will be done automatically at machine-tomachine speed, it will still be a challenge to present all components and interactions of a network, IT enterprise, or cyber ecosystem in a way that enables the humans that oversee these systems to have sufficient situational awareness and to intervene as necessary.

Another challenge is differentiating malicious cyber activity from authorized operations. Operations are highly dynamic, and context is significant; for example, actions that are authorized and appropriate during fiscal end-of-year closeout for a start-up might be malicious activity two weeks before an initial public offering. As a result, current tools have many false positives and false negatives. Many techniques for recognition of malicious cyber activities are also retrospective in nature: these tools look for malicious activities that conform to a known historical pattern (called a signature). Such tools are rendered useless when faced with innovation by an adversary.

A similar challenge exists with malware detection. Signature-based techniques have value because the vast majority of malicious cyber activities reuse software, but by definition they cannot detect the previously unknown or unaccounted for. In addition, polymorphic malware is specifically designed to circumvent signature-based detection. As with intrusion detection, current tools are not designed to deal with unanticipated methods.

Another difficulty is assessing the limits of the protection element as deployed in a system or network. As with physical security, identifying weaknesses in the cyber environment informs the choice of detection means. For physical security, this may involve better locks or security cameras at weak points. For network security, this might indicate the needed level of detail in system logs or where to install a monitoring system. This assessment is commonly performed by "red teams," but qualified personnel are scarce, and the results vary widely.

To address these challenges, new technologies must be developed that:

Enable robust situational awareness. Systems and networks are highly complex, and device mobility increases complexity. To defend networks and systems, it is necessary to identify all critical assets contained within, when devices have been added or removed, and attributes and anomalies associated with the users. Real-time change detection, including schemes that are flexible enough for dynamic network conditions and that enable comparisons against last known good system states, is essential.

Identify weaknesses in systems. Changes in system configuration, introduction of new applications, or discovery of new techniques may reduce the level of protection or create new vulnerabilities. Tools are required to identify shortcomings in protection measures in near real time, so the situation can be remediated.

Reliably detect malicious cyber activities. Paradoxically, many security tools can detect known malware and previously identified sequences of operations, yet the vast majority of damaging malicious cyber activities still rely on those well-known vectors. Research is needed to determine whether these security tools are ineffective or under-utilized. Regardless of how well they work, these techniques were not designed to detect innovative or unanticipated methods. Additional R&D is required to ensure that the techniques can reliably detect the full range of adversaries' malicious cyber activities and reduce detection time. In particular, tools are needed that can detect zero-day malware and innovative sequences of operations with acceptable levels of false positives and negatives. Behavioral intrusion detection and heuristic tools, which look for anomalies to system baseline activities, offer an avenue of promising research.

Data scientists have recently developed data-mining techniques consisting of scalable mathematical techniques capable of extracting useful information from extremely large data sets. Researchers are learning how to apply these techniques to large volumes of network logs. If successful, this could lead to new, more effective, and quicker detection techniques for malicious cyber activities.[33]

R&D Objectives Near-Term:

- Discover and apply automated tools to map networks, including entities, attributes, roles, and logical relationships between processes and behaviors.
- Develop usable presentation interfaces that allow operators to better anticipate incidents, discover them in progress, and achieve better post-incident response.

Mid-term:

- Use data analytics to identify malicious cyber activities and differentiate them from authorized user behavior with low false positive and false negative rates.
- Apply predictive analysis techniques across a range of potential cyber-threat vectors (e.g., via software or hardware) and determine the probable course of action for each threat method. Predictive analysis supports all four defensive elements: Deter, Protect, Detect, and Adapt.

Long-term:

- Develop automated tools for cyber threat forecasting in order to assess the limitations of protective measures and better inform sensor deployment.

3.4. Adapt

Resilience—the ability of cyber systems and cyber-dependent missions to succeed in the face of malicious cyber activities—is emerging as a critical component of cyber defense strategies.[34] Systems with resiliency continue to perform correctly during and after such activities and recover from adverse effects. To sustain resiliency, systems must also dynamically adapt to changing threats and technologies and withstand malicious cyber activities without substantial damage. This resilience should be embedded in components, systems, and systems of systems (and into supporting lifecycle processes, governance, and operations), so that cyber adversaries are deterred because they perceive that the likely gains from malicious cyber activities are outweighed by the costs.

Preparation for malicious cyber activities can be achieved via protection, supported by detection, and the sharing of threat intelligence information. Effective defense entails the ability to respond, recover, and adjust. Cyber defenders must respond rapidly and effectively to adversary activities, which can range from precisely targeted to global-scale operations. Systems must withstand these events, so that critical mission and operational functions meet minimum performance requirements. When an adversary penetrates a system, response options may include segmentation and isolation (quarantine), fail-over to backup or alternate systems, and hand-off of key functions to entirely different systems or manual processes. Because of the complexity of cyber ecosystems, disrupted functions may require substantial recovery efforts within times determined by the criticality of the functions. Recovery options include autonomic self-repair, restoration from quorum-authenticated backup, and transition to new and secure systems. Adjusting involves cyber defense, systems engineering, and organizational risk management. Ongoing and meaningful threat intelligence and lessons learned from past encounters can help inform cyber defenders' future courses of action. Systems-engineering processes need to apply resilience design principles and make trade-offs among alternative resilience-enhancing technologies to produce more resilient systems and missions. Security should be viewed not as a state of perfection to be achieved and maintained, but rather as a flexible, ongoing process of self-evaluation and informed actions, adjusting to the threat as it evolves.

Mature resilience leverages existing approaches for recovery from natural and other non-malicious incidents, whereas emerging resilience design principles and methods take into consideration adversary-directed actions. These include design principles applied to enterprise information technologies and to internal industrial control systems; forensic analysis methods to extract observables and indicators to guide future courses of action from an existing cyber playbook; automated reconfiguration and recovery mechanisms (oriented toward enterprise IT); deception environments to obtain threat intelligence and misdirect adversaries; and research in trusted foundations, fault tolerance,[35] and adaptive defenses.

Challenges

As cyber security technologies are integrated into complex systems and systems of systems, responses often have unforeseen dependencies and coupled interactions. Developers and users need visibility and insight into these system behaviors, as well as analytic techniques and response pathways that maintain clarity and trust and avoid unintended consequences.

Modern IT systems were often designed according to decades-old principles developed when compute cycles and memory were expensive resources that had to be conserved at the expense of other concerns—including cybersecurity. Today, compute cycles and memory are comparatively cheap, so new design principles are needed that take into consideration ongoing cybersecurity research, the persistence of legacy systems, and the continued adoption of disruptive technologies (e.g., IoT). While comparatively cheap compute cycles and storage establish new opportunities for each of the defensive elements, the opportunities for adaptation and resilience are particularly striking. Ongoing cybersecurity research is exploring new clean-slate design approaches, including new hardware architectures that eliminate broad classes of exploitable vulnerabilities by explicitly maintaining the distinction between executable code and data, and new software that introduces diversity among instances of applications. Some approaches are inspired by biological immune systems, creating cyber systems that continue to function in the face of malicious cyber activities and acquire immunity to new methods by learning from past compromises. Systems designed with these clean-slate approaches will continue to interact with legacy systems and technologies, so new design principles must consider the need to achieve resilience in heterogeneous systems that contain suspect components.

Another challenge comes from the increasing use of autonomous systems, which must also be able to support response, recovery, and adjustment with little or no interaction with (or even knowledge on the part of) cyber defenders. Further, adversaries might co-opt or exploit autonomous functions, and the machine learning that underlies them. The implications of autonomy must be considered as resilience design principles and technologies are created.

Multi-scale risk governance presents technical challenges to current cyber defense activities. Decisions that increase, decrease, or shift factors that contribute to risk are made at many levels and at multiple scales. Decisions made at one level can affect other levels in complex and not always obvious ways. Technical approaches are needed to identify and understand risk dependencies and explore the resulting decision space. Another challenge is that the time within which decisions must be made and implemented continues to shrink. In this ever-tightening risk management cycle, information sharing and coordination among decision makers becomes increasingly crucial.

Therefore, to improve the overall ability of systems to adapt, R&D activities should improve the capacity of systems, enterprises, and critical infrastructure to respond, recover, and adjust in three ways:

Dynamic assessment. Measure key properties and attributes of system components and assess potential damage in a trustworthy manner, thereby enabling response and recovery to a known good state. Dynamic assessment means doing this in the context of evolving threat methodologies and system requirements. Focus areas include:

- Real-time digital forensic analysis methods that can provide cyber defenders with insight and understanding of the tactics, techniques, and procedures employed by adversaries. These include methods and tools for the analysis of digital media, data, devices, and network data, and that apply to newer technologies such as mobile, embedded systems, IoT, and distributed cloud services, as well as traditional IT and industrial control systems.
- Real-time assessment of changes, behaviors, and anomalies to enable cyber professionals and other decision makers to make accurate damage assessments, predict and manage potential effects on operations, and determine when system anomalies indicate malicious activity.
- Discovery and analysis of system components and interdependencies (including those injected by adversaries in supply-chain-based malicious cyber activities) to provide insight into how changes in them can affect missions or business functions at multiple scales and timeframes.

Adaptive response. Provide methods to adjust to actual, emerging, and anticipated disruptions, so that mission and organizational needs can continue to be met, while unintended consequences and adversary return-on-investment are minimized. These methods will support risk trade-offs in homogeneous enterprise systems in the near-term, and integrated heterogeneous cyber-physical systems in the midterm. In the long term, they will enable integrated resilient architectures that are optimized for the ability to absorb shocks and speed recovery to a known secure operable state. Focus areas include:

- Autonomous reconfiguration and movement of resources to enable changing cyber assets to be marshaled and directed in order to create a defensive advantage.
- Transparent direct remediation and indirect mitigation of damage. Direct remediation mechanisms isolate damaged or compromised components and systems and provide (via alternate mechanisms, if necessary) essential functionality transparently to end users. Direct remediation will thwart irreparable harm to assets (e.g., destruction or indeterminate corruption) and degradation of critical operations. Indirect mitigation includes recovering, repairing, reconstituting, or replacing potentially compromised components, information flows, or systems, and applying supply chain analysis and reverse engineering so that components can be identified and at scale.
- Application of social science for security, including manipulation of adversary perceptions of cyber effects (e.g., via denial and deception techniques) in order to influence the adversary's knowledge of, and confidence in, the effectiveness of their cyber operations.

Coordination at multiple scales. Provide methods to manage risks at multiple scales (component, device, system, systems of systems, enterprise, or international coalition) and enable comprehensive and collective responses to specific types of malicious cyber activities, such as DDoS attacks. These methods support the collection of threat intelligence in the near-term, coordination of defensive activities in the mid-term, and negotiation and orchestration of collective defenses in the long-term. Focus areas include:

- Collection and production of fused, multi-source threat intelligence and information sharing that can provide cyber defenders with accurate risk assessments, accomplished by means such as privacy-preserving data analytics.
- Orchestrated autonomous or semi-autonomous defensive activities to counter system destabilization (e.g., cascading failures), especially of cyber-physical systems.
- Automated negotiation and orchestration of recovery and resilience courses of action to enable cyber defenders to avoid system destabilization or adversarial manipulation, including during large-scale adversary cyber operations (e.g., large-scale DDoS operations).

- Federated coordination of cyber defenses across organizational boundaries. This includes both technical and social science approaches, such as for decentralized command and control, "no fault" discussions for complex diagnostics, and lessons-learned activities.

R&D Objectives

Near-term:

- Develop the technologies and techniques that enable critical assets to adjust and continue operating acceptably, despite adversary actions.

Mid-term:

- Establish methods to achieve the timely recovery of functionality of inter-dependent systems even while adversary activity continues.

Long-term:

- Build adaptive effective collective defenses informed by predictive analysis that minimize adversary-imposed effects, as well as unintended effects caused by defender actions.

4. EMERGING TECHNOLOGIES AND APPLICATIONS

The previous section defined four elements for effective cybersecurity. These elements are universally applicable and are needed to achieve cybersecurity in all technical contexts. The details for providing these elements may differ depending on the specific context.

This section reviews emerging technologies and identifies R&D priorities associated with that specific technical context. The examples have economic and national security implications, but the list is not exhaustive. Similar analysis can and should be performed for any technology—new, old, or emerging.

Cyber-Physical Systems and the Internet of Things

Cyber-Physical Systems (CPS) are smart, networked systems with embedded sensors, processors, and actuators that are designed to sense and interact with the physical world (including human users) and support real-time, guaranteed performance in safety-critical applications. CPS systems are an increasing part of all national critical infrastructures, finding new applications of CPS technology to improve everyday life and even transforming views of a society and community.

Very early examples of CPS are SCADA (supervisory control and data acquisition) systems that used dedicated communication channels to enable remote control of large industrial equipment. These early systems were very specialized proprietary systems, separated from the Internet and its risks, and used for remote control of, for example, electrical generators and power transmission and distribution. The economic advantages of the Internet and increasing functionality of commodity networking and information technology, however, incentivized re-architecting SCADA systems, unfortunately now raising cybersecurity concerns.

SCADA systems today are no longer walled-off from the threats of the Internet or vulnerabilities in networking and information technologies. Cybersecurity risks now affect the safety and availability of the services provided by critical infrastructures. The threats include purposefully coordinated existential threats to national critical infrastructures.

The emerging industry of IoT is equally affected. IoT refers to physical devices with electronics and software that can be sensed, controlled, and easily interoperated over the Internet. These devices have become the staple of home automation, especially Internet-controllable home lighting, heating, cooling, and security systems. The *2014 NSTAC Report to the President on the Internet of Things* projected a staggering 26-to-50 billion IoT devices will be deployed in manufacturing, business, and home applications by 2020.[36] Cybersecurity will be a daunting challenge at this unprecedented scale with low-end commodity networked devices in many diverse applications.

Cybersecurity risks to the safety of IoT and CPS systems, if unaddressed, will impede and block their adoption by society, preventing the full benefits of this technology from being realized for national priorities.

Cloud Computing

The last decade has seen an expansion of computing onto new kinds of platforms, bringing along with it an expansion of new cybersecurity threats. Commercial cloud computing is one such new platform. In cloud-computing platforms, a service provider maintains a large computing and storage infrastructure in one or more data centers and rents the use of this infrastructure to users, who access it over the Internet.

Cloud-computing platforms have all the cybersecurity concerns of traditional systems where each user maintained their own entirely separate computing infrastructure, in addition to new concerns stemming from the sharing of computing infrastructure in the cloud.

Cloud-computing platforms typically use virtualization to execute computation owned by different users on the same shared hardware and software infrastructure. Virtualization is a technique that supports the illusion that each user has an exclusive use of the computer, when in reality one computer may be splitting its time serving several users. Adversaries can potentially exploit flaws in virtualization to pierce this illusion to access or infer other users' data. The potential to exploit these flaws, coupled with the high degree of network connectivity between computers in a data center, increases the threat that a single adversary armed with the knowledge of a relatively small set of exploitable flaws might harm many customers.

Cloud computing will benefit from broad advances in cybersecurity research in each of the four elements, but targeted research to assess, measure, and verify the protections provided by virtualization techniques will be required for a complete picture.

High Performance Computing

High performance computing (HPC) is essential to the Nation's economic competitiveness, scientific discovery, and national security. In July 2015, EO 13702 established the National Strategic Computing Initiative (NSCI), a whole-of-government effort to advance the full range of HPC technologies and extend HPC access to new business and scientific domains. The NSCI also envisions collaborative efforts with academia and the private sector to complement Federal investments, resulting in a whole-of-nation effort.

Advancing the efficacy and efficiency of HPC cybersecurity controls has been identified as a key technology goal for the NSCI. Like cyber-physical systems, access to supercomputers and networks has traditionally been tightly controlled through physical measures. HPC applications were often designed to operate in a serial fashion, requiring unfettered access to all the computing resources to maximize their computing power. Security controls consumed precious compute cycles without contributing directly towards the task at hand, so their application was relatively limited. HPC network access has become commonplace, as new applications emerge leveraging massive scientific data sets collected by sensors or scientific instruments, and new HPC systems support execution of applications in parallel. This new complexity has heightened HPC security requirements, while the existing pressure to maximize performance remains. New research is needed to determine whether traditional security mechanisms will be effective for the next generation of HPC systems called for by the NSCI, without incurring undue financial costs or performance degradation. If traditional mechanisms are ineffective or inefficient, new technologies will be needed to avoid the consequences of inadequate security (e.g., loss of confidentiality, integrity, or availability, or destruction of data).

Autonomous Systems

Technologies for autonomous systems and components are maturing and their security implications have been raised often. Research challenges for autonomous systems include manipulation of machine learning algorithms and resulting effects on resilience. In the near-term, semi-autonomous systems provide functionality; complete autonomy will largely be moderated by humans in the loop and the emphasis will be on IT management (e.g., performance optimization) and security (e.g., automated response). The mid-term will see semi-autonomous systems of systems that integrate cyber-physical systems and IT (e.g., self-driving vehicles), and autonomy will be moderated not by humans in the loop, but by the ability to orchestrate the system. The long-term will see largely autonomous systems of systems that integrate cyber-physical systems and IT at multiple scales and with varying degrees of autonomy, ranging from micro-robotic swarms to smart cities.

Mobile Devices

Traditionally, users and administrators accessed computers from terminals, system consoles, and desktop workstations. While laptops allowed some mobility, network access usually required a physical connection such as a telephone or Ethernet jack. These constraints have been shattered by the introduction of wireless networking and ubiquitous handheld devices (e.g., smart phones and tablets). BYOD and teleworking initiatives have accelerated these trends. Further, there are more stakeholders involved in achieving security today, including component and device manufacturers, operating system designers and developers, application developers, cloud storage providers, and network providers. While many of the broad advances in cybersecurity technologies will apply to these devices, mobility creates new challenges for protection (e.g., secure update), detection, and situational awareness.

5. Critical Dependencies

Advancements in areas on which cybersecurity critically depends are integral to the development of the four elements. The focus here is on the four elements, their relationship with each dependency, and advances that would contribute to attaining the goals of this Plan.

5.1. Scientific Foundations

Developing scientific foundations was a research theme in the 2011 Plan and still remains important for achieving this Plan's goals and objectives. In today's increasingly networked, distributed, and asynchronous world, cybersecurity involves hardware, software, networks, data, people, and integration with the physical world. Vulnerabilities in one part of a complex system are often used by malicious adversaries to exploit other parts in the system. Heuristic methods are inadequate for developing trusted systems that maintain desired functionality and can accommodate evolving technologies and threats. Such methods often are ad hoc, incomplete, and miss important vulnerabilities; the persistent adversary can often exploit the systems that use such assurance methods. Cybersecurity based on the four elements needs sound mathematical and scientific foundations with clear objectives, comprehensive theories (e.g., of defense, systems, and adversaries), principled design methodologies, models of complex and dynamic systems at multiple scales, and metrics for evaluating success or failure.

In the current state of the art, scientifically established and well-understood solutions exist unevenly in various security subdomains. Most techniques are domain- and context-specific, often not validated as mathematically and empirically sound, and rarely take into account efficacy and efficiency. Thus, the state of the practice consists of heuristic techniques, informal principles and models of presumed adversary behavior, and process-oriented metrics. Establishing scientific foundations in the areas below will directly support the goals and objectives for the four elements:

- Formal frameworks for the four elements with quantitative definitions of threats, measurable security assumptions and guarantees, and efficient formal methods for evaluating compositions of systems, defenses, and adversaries.
- Principled design techniques to construct security ecosystems for the four elements with provable or measurable verification and validation of security properties, and characterizations of efficiency.
- Reasoning frameworks to anticipate evolving and disruptive technologies and threats.

5.2. Risk Management

Technologies associated with the four elements *enable* cybersecurity, but *achieving* appropriate levels of security requires more than technology. The application of these technologies requires significant insight into an organization's goals, its abilities and modalities, and the nature of the threats it faces. Risk management is the ongoing process of identifying, assessing, and responding to risk. To manage risk, organizations should understand the likelihood that an event will occur and the resulting impact so they can determine an acceptable level of risk tolerance. This information is essential in making informed investments with scarce cybersecurity dollars.

Risk management is a relatively mature field, with widely accepted processes and a variety of risk models. National Institute of Standards and Technology (NIST) Special Publication 800-39 presents a generally accepted process, consistent with international standards, for information-security risk management at all levels of an organization.[37] The NIST Framework for Improving Critical Infrastructure Cybersecurity presents a flexible framework to help organizations manage and reduce cybersecurity risk, and has been applied across a broad spectrum of organizations in terms of size (including small and medium-sized businesses) and maturity (i.e., differing levels of cybersecurity). These methods can be applied (individually and in coordination) to a variety of trust and governance models.

While risk management practices offer significant value, the return on investment has historically been influenced by complex and decentralized risk governance, uncertainty in risk assessment techniques, and inaccurate cost estimation. The authority, responsibility, and decision-making power for information risk management are often distributed, resulting in a delayed, fragmentary, or uncoordinated response to risks. Uncertainty in risk assessment techniques is compounded by an inability in traditional models to accurately express that uncertainty. The lifecycle costs of security solutions are often underappreciated with respect to operations and management costs and especially for weak solutions.

Advances in risk management are needed to achieve the R&D objectives of the four elements. In particular, integrated cost modeling techniques are needed that incorporate human factors, such as required expertise and ongoing training, and risk models that incorporate information about the known and projected vulnerabilities. In the long term, it is necessary to better inform risk management by integrating modeling, simulation, and exercises into its practice.

5.3. Human Aspects

Experts estimate that 80-90 percent of current cybersecurity failures are due to human and organizational shortcomings.[38] Comprehensive cybersecurity requires understanding the human facets of cyber threats and secure cyber systems. Much research in social, behavioral, and economic disciplines has investigated the human aspects of cybersecurity problems. The field of cybersecurity economics examines adversaries' incentives and the means by which they profit from malicious cyber activities in the real world. The economic analysis of incentives helps explain why individuals and organizations do (and do not) take action to detect and mitigate cybersecurity threats. Social psychologists have investigated the impact of individual characteristics (e.g., age, gender, dispositional factors of personality) and social norms on promoting good practices in cyberspace. Research on persuasion has identified methods to train, incentivize, or encourage users to improve their cybersecurity behavior. Socio-technical investigations have expanded understanding of the role of trust and assurance in secure socio-technical systems as well as deception and adverse intentions in malicious cyber activities. While these are excellent examples of fruitful multi-disciplinary research activities, many opportunities in the economic, human, and social research still exist for improving cybersecurity. Research in the areas below is needed to support the four elements:

- Research in economic ecosystem externalities to enable understanding of the impact of trust and organizational design on cybersecurity decisions, as well as the role of micro- and macroeconomics in the design, construction, and operation of software, hardware, and systems.
- Modeling and social and behavioral experimentation to help identify the strengths and weaknesses of incentive mechanisms to acquire and deploy cybersecurity measures.
- Development of validated sociological models of human weaknesses and strengths for use in analyzing security properties in systems and the respective roles of users, developers, operators, defenders, and adversaries. There is also a need to identify and teach human behaviors that enhance security and identify effective methods to encourage more cyber-secure behavior in the design and operation of IT systems.
- Modeling international norms, rules of engagement, and escalation dynamics of malicious cyber activities to cyber-warfare to enable identification of institutional and structural factors that promote or undermine a secure cyberspace.
- Preventing and detecting insider threats by designing systems, both human and technical, that can better identify insiders doing harm to their organizations in real-time, rather than after the fact as is common today.
- Research in usable security in order to be able to design security techniques that optimize cognitive efficiency.
- Validated modeling and practices for team composition, coordination across teams, and integrated activities between diverse stakeholders in order to greatly increase the effectiveness of collective actions in the four elements.
- Development of validated models of varied adversary motives, responses, and susceptibility to deterrence actions such as denial, attribution, and retaliation. Understanding and anticipating adversary

reaction to defensive actions and discovering their vulnerability to misinformation and confusion would further serve to reverse their asymmetric advantage.

5.4. Transition to Practice

Federal R&D spending in the cybersecurity arena remains a high national priority and ensuring the transition of research into practice is essential to maximizing return on investments. Accelerating transition to practice was a research theme in the 2011 plan and remains an important aspect of the current Plan.

As reported in the June 2014 "Report on Implementing the Federal Cybersecurity Research and Development Strategy," a gap exists between the research community, which focuses on the study and development of new cyber technologies and practices, and the operations community, which acquires system prototypes and implements them in operational environments.[39] Bridging that chasm requires synergistic efforts and investments by both the R&D and operations communities, and it may mean risk-taking for the private sector as it shepherds research results through the commercialization process. The Federal research community should continue activities outlined in the 2011 plan to expand transitions to practice via technology discovery, testing, evaluation and transition, commercialization, and workforce training.

Federal agencies should continue to allocate R&D funding to transition-to-practice activities, such as System Integrator Forums, Small Business Innovation Research (SBIR) activities, and consortium ventures.

Transition to practice is also a social and behavioral challenge. The 2015 Adoption of Cybersecurity Technologies Workshop report noted that "...early engagement among all stakeholders is critical, a technology or best practice needs a champion, developers need to understand user needs and decision-maker concerns, [and] human factors, such as resistance to change, need to be considered by developers, decision-makers and implementers."[40] Further research in these aspects will facilitate the coordination among Chief Information Officers (CIOs), Chief Information Security Officers (CISOs), procurement officers, and Federal IT managers that will be needed to identify, develop, and deploy appropriate technologies.

Streamlining and accelerating the acquisition process for the results of R&D should also remain a priority. Agencies should continue to assess and selectively utilize all contractual instruments at their disposal. For example, Other Transactions (OTs) can provide a mechanism to streamline and accelerate funding of R&D and also allow agencies to reach performers who are typically not engaged in government-funded research. Reducing the time it takes to obtain patents and trademarks will also accelerate technology innovation and development.

Harmonizing technology transfer processes across Federal agencies would also improve the transition of research into practice. For example, there is no uniform approach for the private sector to license technology developed by the government. Streamlining these processes would significantly eliminate some of the obstacles and accelerate the transfer of technology.

5.5. Workforce Development

Developing and retaining the necessary cybersecurity workforce remains a key challenge. People are an essential component of cyber systems and can contribute to their security (or insecurity) in a variety of ways. The success or failure of this Plan depends largely upon three components of the national workforce: cybersecurity researchers, product developers, and cybersecurity professionals.

The growing demand for cybersecurity professionals is well documented, and appropriate efforts are already underway. The National Initiative for Cybersecurity Education (NICE)[41] was established in 2010 to implement recommendations of the Cyberspace Policy Review[42] and Comprehensive National Cybersecurity Initiative.[43] It is leading a robust portfolio of Federal efforts to satisfy the cybersecurity workforce needs of government and the private sector. NICE coordinates government workforce programs in cybersecurity education, training, and workforce development across more than 20 different Federal departments and agencies; collaborates with industry to understand its cybersecurity workforce needs; and engages with K-12 schools and academia to establish innovative curriculum, degree programs, and experiential learning.

To satisfy national needs for a robust and productive workforce, however, the cybersecurity profession must attract and retain talent from previously untapped applicant pools, change the image of the field by celebrating innovations in cybersecurity, and increase the appeal of the field to a diverse audience of workers. Innovative solutions to national cybersecurity R&D

challenges will come from a diversity of perspectives and by fostering the American entrepreneurial spirit.

A critical cornerstone of secure cyber systems is the recognition that cybersecurity is a shared responsibility borne by researchers, developers, administrators, and users. The common image of the cybersecurity professional as a warfighter, computer "geek," or secret operative, however, appeals to only a minority of potential workers that possess or would consider developing cyber skills. Significant pools of talent have opted out of the cybersecurity workforce, creating a lack of candidates for competitive positions and, equally important, potentially hindering innovation through a lack of diversity of perspectives, problem solving skills, and experience.[44] Expanding the applicant pool by engaging women, under-represented ethnic and racial groups, and people with disabilities is essential to meeting the emerging workforce skills gaps. The Nation must promote training, education, and career development opportunities in cybersecurity fields among the current, entering, and re-entering workforce across all sectors to satisfy present and future workforce demand and supply of qualified cybersecurity workers.

One of the recurring themes in this Plan is measuring the efficacy and efficiency of cybersecurity tools and techniques. Developing the capacity for this type of research within the cybersecurity research community is essential to the success of this R&D Plan. Cybersecurity researchers should acquire skills to adopt efficacy and efficiency as essential components for all cybersecurity research and curriculum development.

This Plan emphasizes the importance of reducing vulnerabilities in IT across the board. Vulnerabilities can only be reduced if developers accept cybersecurity as an essential requirement, adopt assurance-based design and development techniques and tool chains, and incorporate sound security update mechanisms. Developing a software development workforce that recognizes the importance of low-vulnerability IT systems and products and has the skills to achieve that goal, is essential to the success of this Plan.

The community of developers and product architects that needs to understand cybersecurity will continue to grow. For example, medical device designers will need to recognize the interconnected nature of their devices and incorporate cybersecurity protections as well. As the range and scope of cyberspace continues to expand, new workforces must be prepared to integrate cybersecurity technologies and concepts into their fields.

5.6. Research Infrastructure

Access to advanced cybersecurity testbeds continues to be a hurdle for researchers. Testbeds are essential so that researchers can use actual operational data to model and conduct experiments on real-world system vulnerabilities and exploitation scenarios in proper test environments. These models and experimental methods must be shared and validated by the research community by giving them access to these test environments. Current experimental analysis tools, however, are often custom built on an ad-hoc basis, experiment by experiment. Stand-alone testbeds in niche areas of cybersecurity abound but do not enable comprehensive experimentation with inputs from a diversity of human and technological sources. Cybersecurity experimentation must include the ability to capture, model, and recreate realistic human behaviors. Current methods fall short of realistically integrating human factors into experiments and accurately quantifying them as a security variable to be tested.

Data repositories exist today, but many are unable to deal with proliferation of massive data sets, do not support semantically rich data searches and have limited data provenance information. Furthermore, static repositories are of limited value for resilience research, where dynamic, agile repositories are needed. Understanding data provenance is crucial for research and enabling others to reproduce research results on other datasets. In addition, researchers lack access to realistic social media and insider threat data to conduct human behavior analyses, in order to refine technical solutions and policies in these areas.

Due to the vast disparities in system requirements, no single testbed can suffice for all types of cybersecurity research. Stand-alone, sector-specific testbeds offer limited support for research experimentation on inter-dependencies. Such testbeds are proprietary and closed to all but a handful of researchers, and are often not Internet-accessible. A broad array of versatile, non-sector-specific testbeds are needed to enable better testing of methods and procedures as well as standards for testbed interconnection to support complex, large scale activities.

Further, research in cybersecurity requires realistic experimental data which emulates insider threat, external adversary activities, and defensive behavior, in terms of both technological systems and human decision making. The integrity and availability of such data sets is crucial to ensuring scientifically reliable results. Data collection, however, must observe all appropriate laws and regulations and should be ethically conducted.[45] There is a substantial lack of vetted, provenance-detailed, and openly available data sets that are needed in order to obtain research reproducibility, an inherent trait of the science of security. Special, one-off relationships with industry partners to acquire access to their proprietary data means that a broader pool of researchers cannot utilize the data or peer review the results.

Cyber-threat data sharing for operational purposes is crucial in the defense against malicious cyber activities. Such data sharing also has vital strategic benefits to enable research of new, effective ways to protect critical information systems. Currently, data owners possessing real, high-fidelity data are reluctant to share such data for government-funded research. Data owners take on risk when sharing their data with researchers—disclosures of events could damage their reputation and impact business or the public. There is also no accepted safe method for data de-identification to implement privacy and confidentiality protections specifically for research. Aggressive de-identification can make data less useful to researchers, while too little precaution could result in an inadvertent disclosure of personal information, proprietary information, or other sensitive data. There is a need for a plan that supports responsible high-fidelity data sharing for innovative cybersecurity research, providing protections (e.g., indemnification, transfer of liability) to those organizations that voluntarily share this data with researchers after applying accepted de-identification methods. Encouraging cyber-related data sharing for government-funded cybersecurity research through appropriate safeguards for subjects of data and protections for data owners would likely stimulate innovative approaches and solutions.

The Federal Government, with industry participation, should expand the scope and fidelity of cybersecurity testbeds in cloud computing, manufacturing, electrical power, transportation, information and networking systems, healthcare, and telecommunications. It should also enable multi-disciplinary experimentation in computer science, engineering, mathematics, modeling, human behavior, sociology, economics, epistemology, and education.

6. Implementing the Plan

This section reviews the roles and responsibilities of Federal agencies, the private sector, universities and other research organizations for implementing the Plan in 2016 and beyond. It describes existing coordination and planning mechanisms within the private and public sectors and outlines priorities for and possible obstacles to advancing cybersecurity R&D.

6.1. Roles and Responsibilities

Research and development funding is a scarce resource, regardless of source. For this reason, it is essential to invest wisely and selectively to avoid research redundancies. This section identifies the respective roles for the Federal Government, private industry, academia, and research organizations and identifies strategies and vehicles for ensuring coordination among sectors. All organizations must comply with applicable laws and ethics of research. Chief Privacy Officers have unique opportunities to help researchers and program managers conduct productive research that protects and enhances civil liberties.

Federal Research Agencies

The Federal Government has a dual role with regards to its support for R&D. It is the primary source of funding for long-term, high-risk research initiatives but also funds near-term developmental work to meet department- or agency-specific requirements or important public goods that industry is not incented to pursue. Achieving and maintaining the appropriate balance between the two is an ongoing process and the appropriate balance point differs for different agencies.

Science agencies, such as the National Science Foundation (NSF) and National Institute of Standards and Technology (NIST), have a leading role in funding cybersecurity R&D to support this Plan. In keeping with their science missions, these agencies focus on basic and longer-term, higher-risk research. Depending upon the agency, the research may be executed in-house, at national laboratories, or in academia via grants, other transactions, cooperative agreements, or contracts. The challenge for these agencies is twofold: identifying and funding the most promising and important R&D initiatives and transitioning this research into practice. Science agencies will utilize this Plan as the foundation for funding decisions but should also adjust their decision-making as cyber policies and threats evolve. Science agencies should embrace and fund multi-disciplinary research, and continue to demand strong scientific methods in all funded initiatives. They should support foundational research, yet also research that produces data that support the efficacy and efficiency of new techniques or practices so as to contribute to the Plan's vision.

Mission agencies primarily fund applied research with a near-term or mid-term horizon to meet immediate and future mission requirements. Mission-specific R&D is often incremental in nature, and agencies should make special efforts to ensure that the desired functionality is not already available from the private sector (nor from other Federal agencies). Research arms of these mission agencies may also support basic and long term research activities with potential to significantly impact agency missions within their portfolio.

Both science and mission agencies should avoid funding near-term R&D unless it is directly related to mission-specific needs or creates public goods that industry is not incented to pursue. Near-term, broadly applicable R&D is best done within private industry, as it is better positioned to shape and respond to market demands.

Government scientists, national laboratories, and Federally Funded Research and Development Centers (FFRDCs) are positioned to perform long-term high-risk research. These organizations exist to perform research that is too sensitive or too risky for the private sector, and are capable of doing this across multiple disciplines.

With these research performers, however, there are only limited paths for transition to commercial practice. Technologies may become products custom-tailored for the government and satisfy specific mission requirements. In order to have impacts outside the government, Federal agencies should make partnerships with industry.

Private Sector

The budgets for commercially-funded cybersecurity research are usually comparatively modest for even the largest IT companies. Private-sector R&D funding typically is internal and focused on product-development goals based on the specific needs of the company as well as on profitability and turnaround time. While companies often have the skills to perform longer-term higher-risk research, the opportunity cost of moving personnel to address these topics is high, even when government funding is available to defray the immediate costs, because longer-term research often benefits the entire industry and not just the company that funded it. Nonetheless, there are opportunities for the R&D activities of the private and public sectors to be synergistic and complementary. A well-functioning cybersecurity research ecosystem must offer several mechanisms for the two to mutually benefit from each other.

Most companies that have laboratories or groups that are actively pursuing R&D and applications of cybersecurity technologies, tools, and methods are from the IT and telecommunications sectors. Cybersecurity, however, is not just a problem of IT and telecommunications: important cybersecurity R&D is underway at companies producing medical equipment, automotive systems, and avionics. Yet other sectors, such as banking, manufacturing, power, and agriculture can bring value to the research space by working with researchers on long-term issues, providing access to real-world data, and supporting research through funding.

Cybersecurity is not only a problem for big companies, but also for small and medium businesses (SMB). While it is unreasonable to expect SMB to have their own research programs, participating in academic or private-sector programs will help focus researchers on the needs of organizations with limited IT capacity.

Opportunity for fruitful collaboration exists in expanding efforts to measure and verify efficacy and efficiency in cybersecurity products and services. Consumers and enterprises need such information for effective and efficient management of their cybersecurity risks. Indeed, there is a growing awareness in the private sector that compliance-based approaches are not working: cybersecurity needs to be integrated into the broader IT environment and focused on addressing the more important business risks.[46] Private-sector product vendors should consider the full range of costs of using cybersecurity solutions, from financial costs to cognitive load on users to innovation-inhibiting practices. Another fruitful partnership opportunity would be to jointly identify pre-competitive research areas in which private-public partnership funding would be most productive.

Academia and Research Organizations

Academia is the leading R&D performer of basic research and longer-term, higher-risk initiatives. It is the source for new ideas in cybersecurity. Academics are strongly encouraged to embrace this Plan's focus on measurable and testable efficacy and efficiency. Where possible, efficacy metrics against open data sets (such as PREDICT[47]) should be provided to enable comparison and evaluation of competing techniques. Use of open data sets also enables reproducibility of experiments, which is a basic tenet in other scientific disciplines. Academic researchers are also encouraged to incorporate strategies for transitioning successful research into practice when developing proposals and initiating research.

Academia also strongly influences research directions through the promotion and tenure process. Academic institutions are strongly encouraged to value multi-disciplinary cybersecurity research, even where publication occurs in non-traditional journals for the field. Institutions are also encouraged to value research with rigorously-defined models and experimental design.

Research organizations and professional societies are a natural partner in these efforts. They produce research strategies, organize conferences, and publish journals. By establishing publication requirements for documented efficacy and efficiency, these organizations can greatly aid and improve scientific rigor in the cybersecurity field (e.g., by publishing detailed results on experiment methods, measurement techniques, and failed research).

International Partners

Existing efforts in science diplomacy and collaborations with international partners provide an opportunity to complement Federal and private-sector R&D efforts in cybersecurity. Cybersecurity is a global concern, and the United States should leverage other countries' cybersecurity R&D investments and vice versa. This Plan should guide discussions in international technical and inter-governmental meetings so that international cybersecurity R&D investments can complement Federal R&D investments.

Coordination and Collaboration

Coordination and collaboration across sectors is essential to avoiding redundant research initiatives. This coordination should occur at several levels: among departments and agencies; among government, private industry, and academia; and among international partners.

The Federal cybersecurity R&D community does engage with industry via many different mechanisms in the form of public-private partnerships. For example, the Trusted Computing Group is a partnership that provides technology for hardware-based cryptography, key repositories, self-encrypting drives, and device authentication. NSF co-funds research with the Semiconductor Research Corporation (SRC) to support the development of secure, trustworthy and resilient semiconductors. Research alliances can draw together industry leaders to address shared cybersecurity problems and to foster strategies for transformative solutions to these problems. Agencies have also used advisory boards to obtain an industry perspective, such as the NIST Information Security and Privacy Advisory Board. The Department of Homeland Security (DHS) has hosted a dozen National Conversations on a Trusted Cyber Future throughout the country to engage industry leaders. Both DHS and the Department of Defense (DoD) have opened offices in Silicon Valley to expand their conversations with technology innovators. The Federal R&D community also has relationships with the private sector in areas such as cognitive systems, big data, social networking, privacy, cryptography, predictive analytics, search, cloud computing, and software. In addition, there is also National Cybersecurity Center of Excellence (NCCoE) FFRDC, sponsored by NIST to accelerate the adoption of secure technologies.

Coordination between departments and agencies is facilitated by the NSTC. Unclassified Federal research and development efforts in networking and information technology are coordinated by the NITRD Program, supported by the National Coordination Office (NCO) for NITRD. Classified research efforts are coordinated by the NSTC's Special Cyber Operations and Research Engineering (SCORE) subcommittee.

6.2. Implementation Roadmap

The coordinated R&D activities of this plan are carried out by a number of Federal agencies with varying missions but complementary roles. Among the agencies, for example, NSF supports academic research, DARPA focuses on high-risk efforts that both prevent and create technical surprise, DoD Service research organizations focus on their respective mission requirements, and DHS supports applied research in the context of homeland security and securing the Nation's critical infrastructures. This arrangement assures that the full spectrum of R&D approaches is represented and engaged.

Accordingly, each agency structures its R&D activities based on its mission and resources. Each agency should, in collaboration with the Office of Management and Budget (OMB), with other White House organizations as needed, and with Congress, incorporate the objectives of this Plan into its research plans and programs as appropriate. Details of R&D carried out by each agency involved are provided by agencies through their appropriate venues, such as agency-specific strategic plans or implementation roadmaps and via appropriate contracting methods such as solicitations or broad agency announcements (BAAs).

The agencies should engage industry and academics through their individual programs, such as BAAs from DARPA and DHS, public working groups from NIST, and program solicitations from NSF. Each year, the NITRD Program compiles and produces a Supplement to the President's Budget (published at https://www.nitrd.gov), which provides highlights of agency activities and research activities in various areas of IT and networking. In the supplement, the Cyber Security and Information Assurance (CSIA) section provides an overview of the ongoing unclassified Federal investment in cybersecurity R&D. The CSIA section provides information about the activities and investments the agencies are pursuing in implementing this Plan. In addition, the agencies should work through NITRD to coordinate their activities under the Plan and reach out to industry and academia to promulgate the Plan via academic workshops and inviting academics and industry representatives to talk with agency representatives.

7. Recommendations

The Federal Government in its entirety can support this Plan and achieve its vision by supporting the following recommendations:

Recommendation 1: Prioritize basic and long-term research in Federal cybersecurity R&D.

Given the increasing value to the Nation created and enabled by the Internet, there should be a higher priority assigned to R&D to protect that value. Current investments in cybersecurity R&D are not keeping pace with the increase in risk, and have not satisfied society's needs for cybersecurity technologies that are effective and efficient.

The cybersecurity R&D community is active and growing. There are numerous annual world-class research conferences where results can be shared among the community. There is a solid base of R&D funding, including substantial Federal R&D funding as well as ongoing commercial R&D investments. The Nation as a whole would benefit from a steady increase in Federal and private-sector cybersecurity R&D, with a particular emphasis on basic research and long-term, high-risk research initiatives. Because basic research and long-term research especially are areas where the private sector is not likely to invest, Federal investments will be important for R&D in these areas.

Within Federal investments in IT R&D in general and cybersecurity R&D in particular, basic and long-term cybersecurity research should be prioritized. As basic research results mature and as long-term research initiatives become applicable to practice, then support for applied and near-term research, relying heavily on private resources, will also be appropriate.

Recommendation 2: Lower barriers and strengthen incentives for public and private organizations that would broaden participation in cybersecurity R&D.

Additional benefits come by augmenting Federal investments with increased private-sector investments in cybersecurity R&D. Continued data collection and study of the benefits expected and realized by the private sector from investment in cybersecurity would help motivate such investments and could identify classes of incentives that might be effective. A better understanding of the ways to incentivize industry to become more secure is as important to the adoption of cybersecurity techniques and measures as the effectiveness of the technologies themselves.

Federal agencies can lower the barriers to entry into the cybersecurity R&D marketplace by funding common research infrastructure (e.g. testbeds and data sets) in order to lower the cost of entry for small businesses, startup companies, and academic institutions and increase their participation in R&D. These organizations may have game-changing cyber security ideas but lack the financial assets to fund realistic design, modeling, and experimentation using relevant data.

Policymakers should review proposed laws, treaties, and regulations to understand how they impact ethical[48] cybersecurity R&D and consider engaging with relevant stakeholders to modify existing laws and regulations that may inhibit it.[49]

Recommendation 3: Assess barriers and identify incentives that could accelerate the transition of evidence-validated effective and efficient cybersecurity research results into adopted technologies, especially for emerging technologies and threats.

Streamlining the technology transition process for Federally-funded research would encourage more private-sector companies to participate in R&D and transition their technologies. Federal agencies should work towards creating a suite of standardized licensing or other intellectual property agreements that could be selected to facilitate technology transfer for Federally-funded projects.

Utilizing the full range of tools that are in place to create more flexible and attractive technology transfer terms would encourage and enable the public to access and business to leverage government-funded research, including for commercialization.

Recommendation 4: Expand the diversity of expertise in the cybersecurity research community.

Cybersecurity needs extend beyond technology, requiring deep understanding of the human facets of cyber threats and secure cyber systems. To accelerate progress, the skills of traditional cybersecurity researchers should be augmented with expertise from social, behavioral, and economic disciplines.

Multi-disciplinary research should be promoted by funding agencies and by research institutions. Agencies should ensure that grant solicitations and grant review processes are open to multi-disciplinary proposals. Research institutions should ensure that advancement (e.g., tenure) decisions value multidisciplinary research successes and publication in nontraditional journals and conferences equally with traditional tenure criteria.

Recommendation 5: Expand diversity in the cybersecurity workforce.

Diversity encompasses race, gender, ethnic group, age, personality, cognitive style, education, background, and more. Reframing the image of a cyber professional to be a more inclusive one would increase the talent pool, foster critical cyber skills among a wider swath of individuals, and promote a healthier, more culturally-sensitive workplace. A more diverse workforce can provide a richer set of perspectives and innovative solutions to problems. Research is needed to find ways to make cybersecurity a more attractive career option for many people and introduce greater diversity into recruiting and retention practices. Community-focused education campaigns should inform the public about the importance of cybersecurity and promote greater awareness and motivate young people to seek cybersecurity careers. Current professionals in the field should be encouraged to mentor and demonstrate the positive impacts their careers have in the social, economic, and national security sectors as well as the communities in which they work and live.

Harnessing the talent of an inclusive workforce with people of all backgrounds who are diverse in thought, experience, and skills is essential to enabling innovation and creative discovery. Organizational leaders should take measures to foster an inclusive workplace climate in cybersecurity to attract and recruit new talent, maximize employee engagement, and improve employee retention.

The Federal agencies should work with cybersecurity stakeholders to promote the visibility of cybersecurity careers and increase mobility of cybersecurity professionals across government, industry, and academia.

ACKNOWLEDGMENTS

The Cybersecurity Research and Development Strategic Plan Working Group is grateful for everyone who provided input to this Plan. We recognize three contractors who each wrote important subsections, edited subsections, and provided extensive comments on the whole Plan: Nancy Forbes (for NITRD), Brendon Gibson (for DHS), and Vipin Swarup (for DoD). We also acknowledge the timely and thoughtful feedback we received from these reviewers: Marjory Blumenthal, Deb Bodeau, Megan Brewster, Rob Cunningham, Steve Fetter, Gabbi Fisher, Ben Flatgard, Erwin Gianchandani, Heather King, Jim Kirby, Paul Lopata, Marianne Swanson, Paul Timmel, Ralph Wachter, Cynthia Wright, and Heng Xu.

ABBREVIATIONS

BAA	Broad Area Announcement
CISR	Critical Infrastructure Security and Resilience
CPS	Cyber-Physical System
CSIA	Cyber Security and Information Assurance
DDoS	Distributed Denial of Service
DHS	Department of Homeland Security
DoD	Department of Defense
FFRDC	Federally Funded Research and Development Center
HPC	High Performance Computing
ICT	Information and Communications Technology
IoT	Internet of Things
IT	Information Technology
NICE	National Initiative for Cybersecurity Education
NIST	National Institute of Standards and Technology
NITRD	Networking and Information Technology Research and Development
NCO	National Coordination Office

NSF	National Science Foundation
NSTAC	National Security Telecommunications Advisory Committee
NSTC	National Science and Technology Council
NSTIC	National Strategy for Trusted Identities in Cyberspace
OT	Other Transactions
OSTP	Office of Science and Technology Policy
PPD	Presidential Policy Directive
PREDICT	Protected Repository for the Defense of Infrastructure Against Cyber Threats
R&D	Research and Development
SRC	Semiconductor Research Corporation
STEM	Science, Technology, Engineering, and Mathematics
S&T	Science and Technology
VPN	Virtual Private Network

APPENDIX A—CYBERSECURITY ENHANCEMENT ACT TECHNICAL OBJECTIVES

The *Cybersecurity Enhancement Act of 2014* was a major impetus for the development of the Plan. In addition to directing development of Plan and setting a deadline for its publication, the Act included a list of technically-oriented cybersecurity objectives for consideration in the Plan. The list of objectives is reproduced below with a mapping of each objective to parts of the Plan.

Objectives

A. How to design and build complex software-intensive systems that are secure and reliable when first deployed;

Ensuring that software and hardware are designed and implemented to minimize the number of vulnerabilities is a core tenet of the Protect element as defined in the Plan. A key long-term R&D objective for this element is the creation of development tool chains that efficiently produce software with only 1 percent of the vulnerabilities appearing in current COTS products:

> Obtain tool chains that support development of software with one defect per hundred thousand lines of code with a relative efficiency metric of 90% for productivity and system performance (i.e., systems with 1% of the defects in current systems that take no more than 10% longer to implement and run up to 10% slower).

B. How to test and verify that software and hardware, whether developed locally or obtained from a third party, is free of significant known security flaws;

Two aspects of this objective are incorporated into the Protect element in the Plan. To enhance the security of existing code bases, the Plan prioritizes the development of efficient and effective static and dynamic software analysis tools. Researchers and consumers alike can apply these tools to open source code bases, and they are an important component of the software developer tool chains. To ensure that the products deployed are in fact the genuine article, the Plan also highlights the importance of objective measures for supply chain security.

In addition to the discussion in the text, the Plan establishes a mid-term R&D Objective to create static and dynamic analysis tools that reduce the number of vulnerabilities to 10 percent of the vulnerabilities appearing in current COTS products:

> Create tools for static and dynamic analysis that reduce vulnerabilities in traditionally developed code bases to one defect per ten thousand lines of code (i.e., develop testing tools that are sufficiently powerful to reduce the number of vulnerabilities in new and legacy code bases by a factor of ten).

C. How to test and verify that software and hardware obtained from a third party correctly implements stated functionality, and only that functionality;

The Plan addresses this objective within the Protect element, under verify security and verify authenticity.

D. How to guarantee the privacy of an individual, including that individual's identity, information, and lawful transactions when stored in distributed systems or transmitted over networks;

The Plan addresses this objective within the Protect element's security controls theme. Cryptography provides effective and efficient methods for safeguarding privacy and protecting confidentiality in a broad range of current systems and environments. In addition to existing mechanisms, this Plan highlights the importance of lightweight cryptography to support IoT and other resource constrained environments, the Plan also highlights the importance of developing efficient privacy-preserving cryptographic mechanisms for particularly sensitive applications. The Plan identifies these advances as a near-term objective:

> Make cryptographic tools and techniques available for constrained environments (e.g., lightweight cryptography), privacy-sensitive applications (e.g., private databases), and lifetime confidentiality (e.g., quantum-resistant cryptography)

E. How to build new protocols to enable the Internet to have robust security as one of the key capabilities of the Internet;

Ensuring that systems and protocols are designed to minimize the number of inherent weaknesses is a core tenet of the Protect element as defined in the Plan, and includes technologies such as correct computation and designing for correct operation of partially compromised systems.

F. How to determine the origin of a message transmitted over the Internet;

Cryptographic authentication is the fundamental technology for verifying the source of a message. The Protect element includes both authentication and cryptographic security controls. The Detect element can facilitate determining origin and is most effective when considered in advance of designing systems.

G. How to support privacy in conjunction with improved security;

This Plan is focused on development of elements for cybersecurity as traditionally defined: confidentiality, integrity, and availability. Achieving privacy R&D goals will be directly addressed in a forthcoming privacy and confidentiality strategy under development within NITRD.

While privacy R&D falls outside the core of this Plan, the Plan recognizes cybersecurity controls as essential to identify and mitigate privacy risks throughout the development life cycle of these controls. The Plan also postulates that security and privacy are not inherently in at odds with each, but recognizes that some security controls have implications for privacy. The Plan encourages developers of new cybersecurity controls to evaluate and document any implications for privacy and confidentiality.

H. How to address the problem of insider threats;

This Plan does not explicitly differentiate between threats from insiders and external entities, jointly referring to them as "adversaries". While the insider's authorized access would simplify some activities, once the external adversary initially gains access they assume the authorizations of some user or process, essentially achieving the insider's initial state. The advanced security controls and reduction in vulnerabilities envisioned by the Protect element would limit lateral movement by all adversaries. The Detect element is more transformative; it identifies anomalous user behaviors or operates without relying on predefined attack signatures. Since insider malicious cyber activities may be constructed solely from authorized actions, this enhancement would significantly improve detection of insider threats.

I. How improved consumer education and digital literacy initiatives can address human factors that contribute to cybersecurity;

Three parts of the workforce are identified as a dependency for this Plan: cybersecurity professionals; software and hardware developers; and cyber-physical product developers. The National Initiative for Cybersecurity Education (NICE) is the national program office for cybersecurity education, and for satisfying the cybersecurity workforce needs of the government and industry. The Plan also highlights the importance of education and literacy for software and hardware developers with respect to potential supply chain vulnerabilities. The Plan challenge academia to ensure that the next generation of product developers is fully versed in cybersecurity technologies. The Plan also notes the importance of cybersecurity education for product developers in manufacturing, power generation, and other critical infrastructure where IT is now integrated into components.

Cyber education and literacy are not the only means for addressing the human aspects of cybersecurity. The user assumption in Section 2 states that users will minimize efforts that do not directly contribute to the task at hand. Cyber-literate users may still reject cybersecurity tools (such as multi-factor authentication) due to the level of effort imposed by their use. In order to increase their acceptance and adoption, The Plan recommends research in social, behavioral, and economic sciences to enhance and document the efficiency of cybersecurity tools, especially their ease of use.

J. How to protect information processed, transmitted, or stored using cloud computing or transmitted through wireless services;

Protection of information in cloud computing, wireless services, or other networked applications is addressed within the Protect element by the inclusion of cryptography within security controls. Cloud computing is also highlighted in the Section 4, Emerging Technologies and Applications.

K. Include additional objectives the heads of the applicable agencies and departments, in coordination with the head of any relevant Federal agency and with input from stakeholders, including appropriate national laboratories, industry, and academia, determine appropriate.

This Plan incorporates additional objectives under the Deter and Adapt elements. The Deter element supports Federal, state, local, and tribal government roles (e.g. law enforcement) and recommends that system and network owners establish the efficacy of their overall defensive measures. The Adapt element incorporates two additional components of the NIST Cybersecurity Framework for Critical Infrastructure: Respond and Recover.

APPENDIX B—NIST CYBERSECURITY FRAMEWORK CORE

In 2014, NIST published the Framework for Improving Critical Infrastructure Cybersecurity. The NIST Cybersecurity Framework Core defines five functions (Identify, Protect, Detect, Respond, Recover), while this Plan defines four elements (Deter, Protect, Detect, and Adapt). The differences between the NIST functions and this Plan's elements are a consequence of the different scope and objectives associated with these documents, and do not introduce any incompatibility between these efforts. This Appendix provides a map between common parts and identifies differences due to scoping.

The Identify function and Deter element do not have exact complements in the two documents.

The Identify function in the NIST Framework establishes organizational understanding to support management of cybersecurity risks. The activities in the Identify function are foundational for achieving cybersecurity in practice, and must be factored into the design processes described within the Protect element. However, these techniques are more closely related to Risk Management, as described in the Critical Dependencies section of the Plan.

The Deter element describes technologies required to support deterrence through imposed costs on the adversary, such as legal prosecution and economic sanctions. Deterrence through imposed costs is the domain of Federal, state, and local authorities, and falls outside the scope of improving critical infrastructure cybersecurity. The remainder of the Deter element envisions technologies that measure an adversary's level of effort to ensure that costs outweigh the value of gains. While these technologies could be considered when implementing the Framework's Protect function, they do not provide protection by themselves.

The Framework's Protect and Detect functions map directly to the defensive elements with the same names in this Plan. The technologies this Plan seeks to develop would contribute directly to establishing or enhancing these functions.

The Framework's Respond and Recover functions map into a single element in this Plan: Adapt. The Respond function supports the ability to contain a cybersecurity incident, while Recover supports the ability to restore operations after the event. The Adapt element in this Plan envisions automated tools that contain incidents, continue or restore operations during incidents, and adjust the environment to preserve security and operational continuity in the face of ongoing or anticipated malicious cyber activities. Such automated tools demand integration of the respond, recover, and adjust components, so separate elements were not appropriate.

APPENDIX C—PPD-8: NATIONAL PREPAREDNESS

As described below, this policy complements PPD-8 on National Preparedness of March 30, 2011.

Cyber preparedness is an essential part of the National Preparedness System across the prevention, protection, mitigation, response, and recovery mission areas established by PPD-8. By integrating cyber and traditional preparedness efforts, the Nation will be ready to manage incidents that include both cyber and physical effects. The advances in science and engineering envisioned by this Plan will contribute to national preparedness and support the National Incident Management System, when activated.

To clarify the contributions of the four elements described in this Plan, a mapping to the five mission areas in PPD-8 is provided below.

In PPD-8, prevention "refers to those capabilities necessary to avoid, prevent, or stop a threatened or actual" attack. Prevention operations are a subset of those operations that fall within the threat response category of efforts as defined in Section 2.D of this policy and are principally a government responsibility. The attribution technologies within this Plan's Deter element are a key enabler for threat response in the cyber or non-cyber domains. The Detect element contributes to PPD-8 prevention capabilities.

In PPD-8, protection "refers to those capabilities necessary to secure the homeland against...manmade or natural disasters." Both physical and cyber protection activities are needed to secure key IT facilities and services from malicious cyber activity. The technology objectives detailed in this Plan's Protect element contribute directly to this goal.

In PPD-8, mitigation "refers to those capabilities necessary to reduce loss of life and property by lessening the impact of disasters [and includes]...efforts to improve the resilience of critical infrastructure [and]...risk reduction for specific vulnerabilities...." While this term is sometimes used in context of immediate network defense, under PPD-8, mitigation refers only to sustained risk management efforts intended to reduce the probability or lessen the impact of an incident. Risk management is highlighted as one of the Plan's critical dependencies, but is not one fop the four elements.

In PPD-8, response "refers to those capabilities necessary to save lives, protect property and the environment, and meet basic human needs after an incident has occurred." Response activities include the execution of emergency plans and actions to support short-term recovery. In this Plan, response is one of the integrated components of the Adapt element.

In PPD-8, recovery "refers to those capabilities necessary to...rebuilding infrastructure systems [and] ...restoring health, social, and community services...." In the cyber context, recovery is a follow-on activity to response, leading to the full restoration of the affected services and capacities. In this Plan, recovery is one of the integrated components of the Adapt element.

End Notes

[1] "S&T" refers to a broad set of disciplines in Science, Technology, Engineering, and Mathematics (STEM).

[2] Non-malicious.

[3] "Socio-technical" refers to the human and social factors in the creation and use of technology. For cybersecurity, a sociotechnical approach considers human, social, organizational, economic and technical factors, and the complex interaction among them in the creation, maintenance, and operation of secure systems and infrastructure.

[4] In this document, "information technology" is intended broadly to include networking and communications, and may be thought of as interchangeable with "information and communications technology," or ICT.

[5] The Morris worm of November 2, 1988 was one of the first computer worms distributed via the Internet. It was the first to gain significant mainstream media attention. It also resulted in the first felony conviction in the United States under the 1986 Computer Fraud and Abuse Act. It was written by a graduate student at Cornell University, Robert Tappan Morris.

[6] Malicious cyber activity is defined as activities, other than those authorized by or in accordance with U.S. law, that seek to compromise or impair the confidentiality, integrity, or availability of computers, information or communications systems, networks, physical, or virtual infrastructure controlled by computers or information systems, or information resident thereon.

[7] "Risk Nexus: Overcome by Cyber Risks?" The Atlantic Council, Pardee Center for International Futures, and Zurich Insurance Group, April 2015. http://www.atlanticcouncil.org/cyberrisks/.

[8] Evidence is meant to inform and drive both research and practice; it can take forms such as subject-matter-expert opinions, qualitative evidence, models of protection from defined threats, empirical evidence, and mathematical proofs.

[9] https://www.whitehouse.gov/sites/default/files/microsites/ostp/fed_cybersecurity_rd_s trategic_plan_2011.pdf.

[10] http://www.gpo.gov/fdsys/pkg/FR-2013-02-19/pdf/2013-03915.pdf.

[11] http://www.gpo.gov/fdsys/pkg/DCPD-201300092/pdf/DCPD-201300092.pdf.

[12] https://www.fema.gov/media-library/assets/documents/25959.

[13] http://www.dhs.gov/presidential-policy-directive-8-national-preparedness.

[14] https://www.whitehouse.gov/sites/default/files/microsites/ostp/PCAST/pcast_cybersecurity_nov-2013.pdf.

[15] This Plan complements the Critical Infrastructure Security and Resilience (CISR) R&D Plan released in November, 2015. The technical advances envisioned by this strategy apply to the cyber-dependent aspects of our critical infrastructure, furthering the priority areas laid out in the CISR R&D Plan. See https://www.dhs.gov/sites/default/files/publications/National%20CISR%20R%26D%20Plan_Nov%202015.pdf.

[16] "PCAST Report to the President and Congress Ensuring Leadership in Federally Funded Research and Development in Information Technology," August 2015. https://www.whitehouse.gov/sites/default/files/microsites/ostp/PCAST/nitrd_report_aug_2015.pdf.

[17] https://www.whitehouse.gov/sites/default/files/microsites/ostp/pcast-nitrd2013.pdf.

[18] https://www.whitehouse.gov/sites/default/files/microsites/ostp/PCAST/pcast_cybersecurity_nov-2013.pdf.

[19] https://www.whitehouse.gov/sites/default/files/rss_viewer/NSTICstrategy_041511.pdf.

[20] http://nvlpubs.nist.gov/nistpubs/FIPS/NIST.FIPS.201-2.pdf.

[21] http://www.gpo.gov/fdsys/pkg/FR-2014-10-23/pdf/2014-25439.pdf.

[22] http://www.dhs.gov/sites/default/files/publications/NSTAC%20Report%20to%20the%20 President%20on%20the%20Internet%20of%20Things%20Nov%202014%20%28updat%20%20%20.pdf.

[23] "Goals" set the overall aims of the Plan and are more generic and all-encompassing in nature than research objectives. "Objectives" in Section 3 are concrete, specific, measurable, and have timelines.

[24] http://www.nist.gov/cyberframework/upload/cybersecurity-framework-021214.pdf.

[25] As of December 2015, 45 applications and operating systems had more than 250 vulnerabilities listed in the Common Vulnerabilities and Exposures (CVE) database. See https://www.cvedetails.com/top-50-products.php?year=0.

[26] For example, the "2015 Verizon Data Breach Investigations Report" states "For two years, more than two-thirds of incidents that comprise the Cyber-Espionage pattern have featured phishing." See http://www.verizonenterprise.com/DBIR/2015/.

[27] For example, in the 2014 Coverity Scan Report, the defect rate is 0.76 per thousand lines of source code for commercial software. See http://go.coverity.com/rs/157-LQW-289/images/2014-Coverity-Scan-Report.pdf.

[28] Described at http://heartbleed.com/ and https://en.wikipedia.org/wiki/Heartbleed.

[29] Shifting adversary attention to hardware or firmware exploits will increase costs to the adversary, so reductions in software vulnerability alone would deny some malicious activity.

[30] For example, the 2015 Verizon Data Breach Investigations Report states, "For two years, more than two-thirds of incidents that comprise the Cyber-Espionage pattern have featured phishing." Available from http://www.verizonenterprise.com/DBIR/2015/.

[31] To overcome multi-factor authentication, adversaries must perform a combination of on- and off-line exploits to obtain each of the authentication tokens (e.g., password, fingerprint, or physical token), or be in control of the system where authentication data is submitted to piggyback on the authentication event (e.g., to cryptographically sign a challenge). Single-factor systems can often be compromised through the single vector.

[32] Mandiant Threat Report, "M-Trends 2015: A View from the Front Lines," February 2015, Pg. 3.

[33] When such techniques mature, agencies leveraging them will need to ensure compliance to the Federal Agency Data Mining Reporting Act.

[34] The term "resilience" means the ability to prepare for and adjust to changing conditions and withstand and recover rapidly from disruptions. Resilience includes the ability to withstand and recover from deliberate attacks, accidents, or naturally occurring threats or incidents.

[35] Byzantine quorum systems ensure the availability and consistency of replicated data sets in the presence of arbitrary faults.

[36]http://www.dhs.gov/sites/default/files/publications/NSTAC%20Report%20to%20the%20President%20on%20the%20Internet%20of%20Things%20Nov%202014%20%28updat%20%20%20.pdf.

[37] http://csrc.nist.gov/publications/nistpubs/800-39/SP800-39-final.pdf.

[38] For example, in a 2014 IBM report, over 95 percent of all (cybersecurity) incidents investigated recognize "human error" as a contributing factor. See http://media.scmagazine.com/documents/82/ibmcybersecurityintelligenc20450.pdf.

[39] https://www.nitrd.gov/PUBS/ImplFedCybersecurityRDStrategy-June2014.pdf.

[40] http://cps-vo.org/node/19093.

[41] http://csrc.nist.gov/nice/index.htm.

[42] https://www.whitehouse.gov/assets/documents/Cyberspace_Policy_Review_final.pdf.

[43] https://www.whitehouse.gov/issues/foreign-policy/cybersecurity/national-initiative.

[44] According to the 2013 report, Agents of Change: Women in the Information Security Profession, women represent just 11% of the cybersecurity workforce. The RSA Conference panel presentation "Building the Bridge Across the Great Minority Cyber Divide" reported that the combined percentage of Hispanics and African Americans in cybersecurity is less than 10% of the workforce. See https://www.isc2cares.org/uploaded Files/wwwisc2caresorg/Content/Women-in-the-InformationSecurity-Profession-GISWS-Subreport.pdf and https://www.rsaconference.com/writable/presentations/file_upload/prof-m04_building-the-bridge-across-the-great-minority-cyber-divide.pdf.

[45] The Menlo Report: Ethical Principles Guiding Information and Communication Technology Research, August 2012, http://www.dhs.gov/sites/default/files/publications/CSD-Menlo PrinciplesCORE-20120803_1.pdf.

[46] World Economic Forum and McKinsey & Co., "Risk and Responsibility in a Hyperconnected World", January 2014.

[47] The Protected Repository for the Defense of Infrastructure Against Cyber Threats. See https://www.predict.org/.

[48] The Menlo Report: Ethical Principles Guiding Information and Communication Technology Research, August 2012, http://www.dhs.gov/sites/default/files/publications/CSD-MenloP rinciplesCORE-20120803_1.pdf.

[49] Cybersecurity Research: Addressing the Legal Barriers and Disincentives. From NSF-funded workshop, see, http://www.ischool.berkeley.edu/research/publications/2015/cybersecurity_research_addressing_legal_barriers_and_disin centives.

In: Federal Cybersecurity
Editor: Cory Medina
ISBN: 978-1-63485-395-8

Chapter 2

TRUSTWORTHY CYBERSPACE: STRATEGIC PLAN FOR THE FEDERAL CYBERSECURITY RESEARCH AND DEVELOPMENT PROGRAM*

Cyber Security and Information Assurance Research and Development Senior Steering Group (CSIA R&D SSG) and the Cyber Security and Information Assurance Interagency Working Group (CSIA IWG)

EXECUTIVE OFFICE OF THE PRESIDENT NATIONAL SCIENCE AND TECHNOLOGY COUNCIL

WASHINGTON, D.C. 20502
December 6, 2011

Dear Colleague:

Today's cyberspace—the powerful, virtual environment enabled by digital infrastructure—provides a bright landscape for commerce, science, education, communication, an open and efficient government, and much more. It also

---

* This is an edited, reformatted and augmented version of a document issued by the National Science and Technology Council, December 2011.

harbors threats to security and privacy that can limit its uses and potential. Recognizing that America's prosperity in the 21st century hinges on rebalancing cyberspace in favor of benefits and against threats, President Obama ordered a top-to-bottom review of the government's cybersecurity efforts. The resulting strategy is detailed in the President's *Cyberspace Policy Review* and establishes innovation—including through game-changing R&D—as one of its pillars. The President's Council of Advisors on Science and Technology (PCAST) in its 2010 review of the Networking and Information Technology Research and Development (NITRD) Program also called for transformational R&D to assure both the security and robustness of cyber infrastructure.

This report, *Trustworthy Cyberspace: Strategic Plan for the Federal Cybersecurity Research and Development Program* was developed by the NITRD agencies and directly responds to the need for a new cybersecurity R&D strategy. As recommended in the *Cyberspace Policy Review's* near-term action plan, *Trustworthy Cyberspace* replaces the piecemeal approaches of the past with a set of coordinated research priorities whose promise is to "change the game," resulting in a trustworthy cyberspace. As called for in the policy review's mid-term action plan, this plan identifies opportunities to engage the private sector in activities for transitioning promising R&D into practice. In addition, and consistent with the PCAST recommendations, it prioritizes the development of a "science of security" to derive first principles and the fundamental building blocks of security and trustworthiness.

I am pleased to commend this Federal cybersecurity R&D strategic plan as part of the Administration's comprehensive effort to secure the future of the Nation's digital infrastructure. I look forward to working with the Congress, the agencies, the private sector, and the public to realize that goal.

Sincerely,

John P. Holdren
Assistant to the President for
Science and Technology Director,
Office of Science and Technology Policy

PREFACE

Cyberspace–the globally interconnected information infrastructure that includes the Internet, telecommunications networks, computer systems, and industrial control systems–is rich in opportunities to improve the lives of people around the world. Assuring continued growth and innovation in cyberspace requires that the public has a well-founded sense of trust in the environment. Increasingly frequent malware attacks and financial and intellectual-property thefts must be addressed in order to sustain public trust in cyberspace but address real threats to national security.

The Obama Administration recognizes the magnitude of what is at stake. The President's *Cyberspace Policy Review*[1] unequivocally states that the Government has a responsibility to address strategic cyberspace vulnerabilities to protect the Nation and to ensure that the United States and its citizens can realize the full potential of the information technology revolution. In fulfilling this responsibility, Federal research agencies joined together to develop a strategic plan for cybersecurity research and development (R&D) that confronts underlying and systemic cyberspace vulnerabilities and takes maximum advantage of the Federal government's unique capabilities as a supporter and champion of fundamental research.

In introducing this strategic plan, we would like to highlight three important principles that guided its development. First, the research must aim at underlying cybersecurity deficiencies and focus on root causes of vulnerabilities–that is, we need to understand and address the causes of cybersecurity problems as opposed to just treating their symptoms. Second, the Strategic Plan must channel expertise and resources from a wide range of disciplines and sectors. Cybersecurity is a multi-dimensional problem, involving both the strength of security technologies and variability of human behavior. Therefore, solutions will depend not only on expertise in mathematics, computer science, and electrical engineering but also in biology, economics, and other social and behavioral sciences. Third, we need enduring cybersecurity principles that will allow us to stay secure despite changes in technologies and in the threat environment. Whether we use desktop computers, tablets, mobile phones, control systems, Internet-enabled household appliances, or other cyberspace-enabled devices yet to be invented, we must be able to maintain and fulfill our trust requirements to ensure our continued security and safety.

This strategic plan describes and prioritizes several research themes worthy of further inquiry, and end-states and capabilities that must be achieved in order to fundamentally improve cyberspace. The Plan does not focus on specific technical problems and challenges, e.g., developing better firewalls or more secure operating systems. Rather, by articulating desired end-states and capabilities, the themes reveal important underlying causes of cybersecurity vulnerabilities. By defining the end-states, rather than the paths to get there, the themes invite a diversity of approaches and encourage innovation across disciplines and sectors. Of course, along the way to achieving these larger solutions, many perennial problems and technical challenges will have to be solved.

Over the last three years, Federal agencies engaged in an intensive round of public discussions, brainstorming, and detailed examinations of cybersecurity-related technical issues in order to develop the research themes that are at the heart of this strategic plan. The process of building the Strategic Plan began with a Leap-Ahead Initiative—set in motion by the White House Office of Science and Technology Policy (OSTP) in April 2008 as a component of the Comprehensive National Cybersecurity Initiative. That effort solicited public input and received more than 230 responses focused on how to change the cybersecurity landscape. These were distilled into five fundamental "game-changing" concepts that were then discussed by over 150 innovators from the academic and commercial sectors at the National Cyber Leap Year Summit held in August 2009 in Arlington, Virginia. Finally, the outcomes of the summit were distilled into the research themes articulated in this strategic plan.

Cybersecurity is a shared responsibility across the public and private sectors. Thus, the execution of this cybersecurity research strategy will require the participation of a broad spectrum of public and private stakeholders. Indeed, much of the U.S. cyber infrastructure is privately held—and many private industries (e.g., financial, healthcare, energy enterprises) have interests in the protection of intellectual property (IP) and the assurance of secure business transactions—so shielding that infrastructure against acts of industrial espionage and securing it against IP theft are critically important to private-sector entities. Similarly, the academic community has interests in a secure cyberspace that enables open collaboration, sharing of data, and protection of the vital infrastructure that supports fundamental research and discoveries.

Critical cybersecurity challenges in national priority areas such as healthcare, energy, financial services, and defense can be confronted by focusing R&D activities within the framework of this strategic plan. In support of national priorities, government agencies are coordinating efforts with partners in research areas that warrant broader support and collaboration. For example, the National Science Foundation (NSF) is supporting basic research into areas such as the science of security, while the Department of Homeland Security (DHS) is focusing on applied research and transition to practice activities. Several agencies, such as NSF, DHS, and DARPA, have already included some of the research themes described in this plan in their recent solicitations. The Federal agencies are also coordinating support for cybersecurity education and activities designed to foster a vibrant cybersecurity R&D community.

Taking advantage of the inherent public-private nature of the problem, the Strategic Plan calls for bringing together researchers, small businesses, and venture capitalists in the creation of technology demonstration forums to showcase technologies that have potential for further prototyping and/or commercialization. This approach allows for maximum implementation flexibility as the challenges evolve with changing technology. The NITRD Program will continue to coordinate the Federal portion of these activities across government agencies.

We are confident that the public-private research activities in this strategic plan will result in new capabilities and technologies that will unlock the full potential of a safe, secure, and reliable cyberspace.

Sincerely,
Douglas Maughan, DHS S&T
William Newhouse, NIST
Co-Chairs
NITRD Cyber Security and Information Assurance Interagency
Working Group (CSIA IWG)

SUMMARY

Trustworthy Cyberspace: Strategic Plan for the Federal Cybersecurity Research and Development Program defines a set of interrelated priorities for the agencies of the U.S. government that conduct or sponsor research and development (R&D) in cybersecurity.

The priorities are organized into four thrusts: Inducing Change, Developing Scientific Foundations, Maximizing Research Impact, and Accelerating Transition to Practice. The thrusts provide a framework for prioritizing cybersecurity R&D in a way that concentrates research efforts on limiting current cyberspace deficiencies, precluding future problems, and expediting the infusion of research accomplishments into the marketplace. The principal objectives of the thrusts include achieving greater cyberspace resiliency, improving attack prevention, developing new defenses, and enhancing our capabilities to design software that is resistant to attacks.

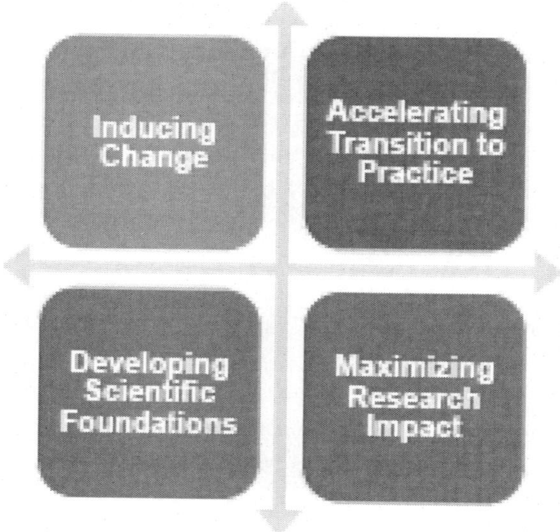

The Inducing Change thrust includes a new priority theme named Designed-in Security, together with the existing themes of Tailored Trustworthy Spaces, Moving Target, and Cyber Economic Incentives. The Designed-in Security theme focuses on developing capabilities to design and evolve high-assurance systems resistant to cyber attacks, whose assurance properties can be verified. Such development capabilities offer the path to dramatic increases in the security and safety of software systems.

Explicit in the execution of this plan is the coordination process across government agencies through the Federal Networking and Information Technology R&D (NITRD) Program and the leadership function of the NITRD Cyber Security and Information Assurance Interagency Working Group (CSIA IWG), the Federal government's principal group for coordinating cybersecurity R&D activities. In conjunction with the White House Office of Science and Technology Policy (OSTP), the NITRD Senior Steering Group for Cybersecurity R&D, and the Special Cyber Operations Research and Engineering (SCORE) Interagency Working Group, the CSIA IWG assures that the execution of this plan by individual Federal research agencies is coordinated, cohesive, and complementary.

1. Why a Strategic Plan?

Today, the nation faces significant challenges in all areas of cybersecurity.[2] The prevalent cybersecurity R&D approaches of incremental, piecemeal efforts driven by the individual interests of researchers or solution providers are not sufficient to respond to present or future threats. A more effective strategy is to establish a coordinated cybersecurity R&D effort (see Section 4.2 "Research Coordination") whose research goals and activities derive from an explicit framework that compels the changes necessary to assure a more secure future in cyberspace. Within the framework, the Federal government has a unique role and responsibility: It must drive fundamental change by investing in the kind of long-term basic research that can improve cyber safety and security for people, computer systems and networks, information, and critical national infrastructures. Government investment in basic research is essential because industry does not have the economic interest or return-on-investment time horizon to make such investments or conduct such research. Government investments in the networking of universities and research laboratories, which gave rise to the worldwide Internet, have paid off many times over for society and individuals around the world. Additionally, this plan identifies areas for fruitful public-private partnerships with a focus on government priorities.

Failure to respond to cybersecurity challenges from a position of strength carries enormous penalties; investing in incremental improvements only allows the consequences of the lack of cybersecurity to grow more severe and provides no real protection against determined adversaries. Cyber criminals and nation-state actors are extremely persistent and cunning: They steal the intellectual property that drives innovation in businesses and the credentials that allow individuals legitimate access to health, financial, communications, and other services. They alter information to impair decision-making and corrupt or commandeer command-and-control systems. They cause harm by compromising cyber-physical systems and by engaging in systemic denial of service. They invade, sabotage, and corrupt networks and systems, and otherwise engage in increasingly disruptive activities. They show talent in adapting their tactics in dangerous ways that can cripple businesses, governments, and global economic and political ecosystems. Without strong leadership and a coordinated strategy to unite public and private entities against these forces, the risks of operating in cyberspace may become untenable for most citizens and enterprises, and may critically impair the operational capabilities and integrity of open governments and civil societies.[3]

2. Objectives

A primary objective of the Federal cybersecurity R&D strategic plan is to express a vision for the research necessary to develop game-changing technologies that can neutralize the attacks on the cyber systems of today and lay the foundation for a scientific approach that better prepares the field to meet the challenges of securing the cyber systems of tomorrow. As a strategic plan, this document provides guidance for Federal agencies, policymakers, researchers, budget analysts, and the public in determining how to direct limited resources into activities that have the greatest potential to generate the greatest impact. The strategic plan profiles R&D areas that span multiple disciplines, surfacing intersections of common interest that hold potential for stimulating collaboration among researchers and technical experts in government, private industry, academia, and international contexts. The strategic plan also offers ideas for decision-makers to consider when deliberating about investments in cybersecurity science and technology in their respective domains. The strategic plan represents the culmination of several years of exploration and examination of cybersecurity issues by government representatives in the NITRD Senior Steering Group for Cybersecurity R&D, the NITRD Cyber Security and Information Assurance Interagency Working Group, and the Special Cyber Operations Research and Engineering Interagency Working Group, as well as by the cybersecurity community. The ideas distilled from the planning process garner widespread support and serve in this plan as waypoints to guide us along a path that can significantly advance the field of cybersecurity.

3. Federal Cybersecurity Research and Development Program Thrusts

The Federal cybersecurity R&D program is characterized by the following strategic thrusts to organize activities and drive progress in cybersecurity R&D:

Inducing Change – Utilizing game-changing themes to direct efforts towards understanding the underlying root causes of known current threats with the goal of disrupting the status quo with radically different approaches to improve the security of the critical cyber systems and infrastructure that serve society.

Developing Scientific Foundations – Developing an organized, cohesive scientific foundation to the body of knowledge that informs the field of cybersecurity through adoption of a systematic, rigorous, and disciplined scientific approach. Promotes the discovery of laws, hypothesis testing, repeatable experimental designs, standardized data-gathering methods, metrics, common terminology, and critical analysis that engenders reproducible results and rationally based conclusions.

Maximizing Research Impact – Catalyzing integration across the game-changing R&D themes, cooperation between governmental and private-sector communities, collaboration across international borders, and strengthened linkages to other national priorities, such as health IT and Smart Grid.

Accelerating Transition to Practice – Focusing efforts to ensure adoption and implementation of the powerful new technologies and strategies that emerge from the research themes, and the activities to build a scientific foundation so as to create measurable improvements in the cybersecurity landscape.

3.1. Inducing Change

The strategic plan advances carefully considered research themes to converge a broad range of research and development activities on delivering technologies that improve the trustworthiness of cyberspace. The purpose of the research themes is to focus research activities on characteristics that are essential to the desired end-states of trustworthy systems. The themes provide opportunities for synergy among researchers with different subject-matter expertise who otherwise might concentrate only on a particular property or behavior of trustworthy systems. As such, the themes provide an operational flavor to research directions.

The cybersecurity research themes in this plan share characteristics that shape, direct, and facilitate a coherent and coordinated R&D agenda. The themes compel a new way of operating or doing business, and give focus to underlying causes in order to bring about change. The themes are fundamentally interdisciplinary, draw upon a number of sciences and technologies, and foster synergy among researchers. The themes encourage an adversarial perspective in the conduct of research and in endeavors that closely examine the security, reliability, resiliency, privacy, usability, and overall trustworthiness of digital infrastructure. With activities and engagements that may span multiple years and require measurable achievements, the themes present a logical path from research to transition, deployment, and cooperation with the private sector.

A cybersecurity research theme may evolve and expand to include more complex topics, as knowledge improves and clarity is gained in matters unclear at the inception of a theme. Likewise, as our understanding of cyberspace matures, there may be a need to add new themes or theme focus areas.

This strategic plan introduces one new Federal cybersecurity R&D theme and expands upon the three themes introduced in FY 2010, which emerged from National Cyber Leap Year[4] activities. In short, the themes are as follows:

Designed-In Security (New Theme) – Builds the capability to design, develop, and evolve high-assurance, software-intensive systems predictably and reliably while effectively managing risk, cost, schedule, quality, and complexity. Promotes tools and environments that enable the simultaneous development of cyber-secure systems and the associated assurance evidence necessary to prove the system's resistance to vulnerabilities, flaws, and attacks. Secure, best practices are built inside the system. Consequently, it becomes possible to evolve software-intensive systems more rapidly in response to changing requirements and environments.

Tailored Trustworthy Spaces – Provides flexible, adaptive, distributed trust environments that can support functional and policy requirements arising from a wide spectrum of activities in the face of an evolving range of threats. Recognizes the user's context and evolves as the context evolves.

Moving Target – Enables us to create, analyze, evaluate, and deploy mechanisms and strategies that are diverse and that continually shift and change over time to increase complexity and cost for attackers, limit the exposure of vulnerabilities and opportunities for attack, and increase system resiliency.

Cyber Economic Incentives – Develops effective incentives to make cybersecurity ubiquitous, including incentives affecting individuals and organizations. Incentives may involve market-based, legal, regulatory, or institutional interventions. Recognizes that sound economic incentives need to be based on sound metrics, including scientifically valid cost risk analysis methods, and to be associated with sensible and enforceable notions of liability and care. Requires advances in understanding the motivations and vulnerabilities of both markets and humans, and how these factors affect and interact with technical systems.

Cybersecurity R&D Themes
Designed-in Security
Tailored Trustworthy Spaces
Moving Target
Cyber Economic Incentives

This strategic plan establishes the four cybersecurity R&D themes to unify a variety of research and development activities by focusing the cybersecurity research community on a common set of problems. The intent of each theme is to delineate the scope of a compelling hard problem in cybersecurity against which there can be a focused Federal investment to inspire and foster new ideas, and to engender innovative, game-changing solutions. The four themes are multiyear challenges to sustain and focus R&D activities over time; there is no requirement to drop a theme to accommodate a new theme. While the four R&D themes give focus to research endeavors with the most promising impact on national cybersecurity issues, they do not obviate the need for agencies to undertake other research activities that are important to their missions.

We recognize that the trustworthiness of cyberspace is not a fixed end-state, but a dynamic state, in which there is a continuous process of defensive adjustments and anticipatory adaptations. Moreover, in cyberspace environments related to national security and military activities, there must be a fundamental assumption that the environment is suspect and that its trustworthiness must be continuously monitored and analyzed. Both the dynamic state of cyberspace trustworthiness and the requirement for operational adaptation serve as a critical backdrop to the discussion of the R&D themes below.

In the sections that follow, the strategic plan identifies and describes the characteristics of the four cybersecurity research themes. Included are perspectives on the types of cybersecurity R&D activities that may engender game-changing technologies and solutions applicable to these paradigms.

Designed-in Security

The Designed-in Security (DIS) theme focuses on designing and producing software systems that are resistant to attacks by dramatically reducing the number of exploitable flaws. Using assurance-focused engineering practices, languages, and tools, software developers will be able to develop a system while simultaneously generating the assurance artifacts necessary to attest to the level of confidence in the system's capabilities to withstand attack.

Over the past ten years, the field has shown substantial progress in methods for detecting flaws in software through static and dynamic analysis, producing checkable proofs that demonstrate that software is free of classes of flaws and proving that algorithms and their implementations have desired properties.[5] This progress gives impetus to the new Designed-in Security research theme, whose intent is to stimulate, accelerate, and focus research in the many disciplines that contribute to the design and delivery of large-scale software systems that require verifiable assurance of the system's resistance to attack.

The DIS research theme focuses on building the capability to design, develop, and evolve high-assurance software-intensive systems predictably and reliably while effectively managing risk, cost, schedule, quality, and complexity. Assurance-focused engineering practices can simultaneously develop a system and the evidence needed to support its assurance case, yielding game-changing reductions in cost and increases in agility and flexibility over existing approaches that focus on after-the-fact assurance. This can also enable rapid evolution and tailoring of systems initially developed using these practices.

A key focus within this theme is on the usability of tools for developing attack-resistant software systems. Improving the usability of tools for specifying, implementing, analyzing, and testing software, and for composing systems of software components, is essential in order to gain their widespread adoption by developers, whose participation is needed in order to change the game. The impact of DIS is intended to extend to the development and evolution of mainstream software ecosystems and infrastructures. Future software ecosystems and infrastructures that employ this cost-effective method for producing and evolving high-assurance systems can lay a new, sound foundation for cyber civilization.

The ecosystem within which DIS-hardened software components and systems operate necessarily includes hardware components. As a holistic approach, the DIS theme may extend to the secure design, fabrication, and testing of hardware in its manufacture and assembly. Implementing techniques to protect and enable secure hardware design and manufacturing processes can contribute to the overall assurance case for systems in terms of both supply chain trust and infrastructure provisioning.

This theme affords intermediate payoffs, given that an assurance case entails reasoning about a diversity of quality attributes (security, safety, reliability, etc.), each of which has its own approaches to creating evidence. This enables a trade-off between complexity in models and programming language for the capability to achieve high levels of assurance. Consequently, as progress is made in the overall program of effort, higher levels of assurance can be reached for more attributes, for more complex systems, and with greater affordance in systems evolution.

The research challenges of this theme include:

- The design of models and techniques to support on-the-fly evidence creation during a systems engineering process
- Mathematically sound techniques to support combination of models and composition of results from separate components
- Analysis techniques (based on model checking, abstract interpretation, semantics-based testing, and/or verification) to enable traceable linking among diverse models and code
- Language design, processing, and tooling techniques that are oriented to achieving high assurance for systems with high levels of capability, modularity, and flexibility
- Team and supply chain practices to facilitate composition of assurance in the supply chain
- Tooling to support information management, configuration management, and developer/ team interaction to support rapid and automatic management of the chains of evidence linking software code, models, analysis results, etc.
- Psychology and human factors for how to build software specification, implementation, verification, analysis, and testing tools that are easy to use and provide positive feedback to users
- Economics to improve motivation for use of tools through measurement of improved reliability and security

Tailored Trustworthy Spaces

Today, cyberspace is composed of subsystems that lack mechanisms to ascertain their security conditions and to participate in creating environments with required trust and provenance characteristics. The absence of mechanisms to establish trust has made cyberspace vulnerable to illicit exploitations. Tailored Trustworthy Spaces (TTS) provide flexible, adaptive, distributed trust environments that can support functional and policy requirements arising from a wide spectrum of activities in the face of an evolving range of threats. A TTS recognizes the user's context and evolves as the context evolves. A TTS enforces the user's chosen level of trust, ranging from a fully anonymous transaction to a trusted transaction with strong attribution and traceable authentication. The user is informed of the levels of trust available and chooses to accept the protections and risks of a particular tailored space. The attributes of each available trusted space must be expressible in an understandable way to support informed choice. The attributes must be made manifest and readily usable to support being customized, negotiated, adapted, and enforced. All parties to the transaction must agree on the level of trust enforced by the underlying infrastructure.

The power of the tailored trustworthy spaces theme lies in the capability to:

- Articulate and negotiate the security requirements of the situation at hand
- Adjust the assurance level on specific security attributes separately
- Establish trust between systems based on verifiable information

The primary goal of the tailored spaces theme is to identify and develop a common framework that supports varying trustworthy space policies and services for different types of actions. These policies and services will provide visibility into rules and attributes of the space to inform trust decisions, a context-specific set of trust services, and a means for negotiating the boundaries and rules of the space. This framework will offer assurance that user requirements are accurately articulated in the TTS policy, that these spaces are truly separate, and that build-up and tear-down of the space is clean and trustworthy.

The challenge of tailored spaces is to provide the separation, isolation, policy articulation, negotiation, and requisite assurances necessary to support specific cyber sub-spaces. Research is required to develop:

- Trust negotiation tools and data trust models to support negotiation of policy
- Type-safe languages and application verification, and tools for establishment of identity or authentication as specified by the policy
- Data protection tools, access control management, and monitoring and compliance verification mechanisms to allow for informed trust of the entire transaction path
- Resource and cost analysis tools
- Hardware mechanisms that support secure boot load and continuous monitoring of critical software
- Least-privilege separation kernels to ensure separation and platform trust in untrustworthy environments
- Application and operating systems elements that can provide strong assurance that the program semantics cannot be altered during execution
- Support for application-aware anonymity to allow for anonymous web access, and platform security mechanisms and trust-in-platform

Focus Area ➡ Wireless Mobile Networks

Current security solutions are often not readily applicable in the mobile wireless context due to size, processing, and power constraints imposed by mobile devices. Yet, in order to achieve end-to-end trusted cyber subspaces, wireless technologies must support TTS capabilities that integrate with TTS capabilities in traditional wired and fixed networks. This focus area highlights the need for robust TTS R&D activities to ensure that the rapidly growing wireless domain can fully benefit from, and participate in, TTS solutions and technologies.

Moving Target

Currently, attackers have the advantage of being able to exploit our systems. The systems we use are deterministic, homogeneous, and static, allowing investments in attack to pay off due to unchanging vulnerability windows. When vulnerabilities endure, attackers have the ability to lie in wait, develop attacks, and compromise systems at their own pace. Moving Target (MT) strategies aim to substantially increase the cost of attacks by deploying and operating networks and systems in a manner that makes them less deterministic, less homogeneous, and less static.

Research into MT technologies will enable us to create, analyze, evaluate, and deploy mechanisms and strategies that are diverse and that continually shift and change over time to increase complexity and cost for attackers, limit the exposure of vulnerabilities and opportunities for attack, and increase system resiliency. The characteristics of an MT system are dynamically altered in ways that are manageable by the defender yet make the attack space appear unpredictable to the attacker.

This game-changing approach challenges the traditional approach, which counsels that adding complexity to our systems also adds risk. Conversely, the complexity of today's computational platforms and analytic and control methods can now be used to frustrate our adversaries. The challenge is to demonstrate that complexity is indeed a benefit and not a liability.

The MT area has its underpinnings in fundamental research in the following supporting or component areas: virtualization, multi-core processing, new networking standards, cryptography, system management, software application development, and health-inspired or evolutionary resiliency and defense methods.

Research is required to:

- Develop abstractions and methods that will enable scientific reasoning regarding MT mechanisms and their effectiveness
- Characterize the vulnerability space and understand the effect of system randomization on the ability to exploit those vulnerabilities
- Understand the effect of randomization of individual components on the behavior of complex systems, with respect to both their resiliency and their ability to evade threats
- Develop a control mechanism that can abstract the complexity of MT systems and enable sound, resilient system management
- Enable the adaptation of MT mechanisms as the understanding of system behavior matures and our threat evolves

Focus Area ➡ Deep Understanding of Cyberspace

To operate effectively as a moving target in cyberspace, we must understand our system state, be aware of our surroundings, know the soundness of the structures on which we rely, and know what is happening around us. Cyberspace is complex, and moving target techniques will increase that complexity. Actions in cyberspace are instantaneous. If we are to manage our moving target capabilities effectively and instantaneously in the face of this complexity, we must greatly enhance our ability to monitor, model, analyze, and understand our own system, the systems in cyberspace with which it interacts, and the threat environment at that point in time. If we are to make these decisions within the tight time constraints of cyber actions, we must greatly enhance the speed of our complex analytics and tighten our feedback loops. Ultimately, we must provide knowledge-driven systems that remove the human from the loop in many system decisions. But for those decisions that do require human decision-making, the combination of high complexity and short processing time strains human cognitive processes, so we must provide novel methods of presenting information, directing attention, and navigating between analytics at different scales. We must also provide capabilities that enable a deep, not just comprehensive, understanding of cyberspace. Our methods must enable us to view the situation from alternative points of view and to get below surface indicators to determine underlying causes and conditions.

Focus Area ➡ Nature-Inspired Solutions

There are many natural systems that are far more complex than our cyber systems but are nonetheless extremely robust, resilient, and effective. The biological immune systems that many organisms use to defend against invaders function remarkably well in distributed, complex, and ever-changing environments, even when subject to a continuous barrage of attacks. They exhibit a wealth of interesting mechanisms that can be the inspiration for many new MT methods for securing cyber systems.

There are several immunological principles, such as distributed processing, pathogenic pattern recognition, multilayered protection, decentralized control, diversity, and signaling, that could result in the development of novel approaches to solve problems of cybersecurity: for example, early and dependable detection and recognition of information attacks, rational utilization of network resources to minimize damage and enable a fast recovery, and development of successful ways to prevent further attacks. With this new awareness of their health and safety, the network and host components can deploy a range of options: They may take preventative measures, rejecting requests that do not fit the profile of what is good; they can build immunological responses to the malicious agents that they sense in real time; they may refine the evidence they capture for the pathologist, as a diagnosis of last resort, or to support the development of new prevention methods.

Cyber Economic Incentives

Cybersecurity practices lag behind technology. Solutions exist for many of the threats introduced by casual adversaries, but these solutions are not widely used because incentives are not aligned with objectives and resources are not correctly allocated.

Secure practices must be incentivized if cybersecurity is to become ubiquitous. Sound economic incentives need to be based on sound metrics, processes that enable assured development, sensible and enforceable notions of liability, and mature cost risk analysis methods. Without a scientific framework, it is difficult to incentivize good cybersecurity practices and subsequently to make a convincing business case for enhanced cybersecurity mechanisms or processes. The projected benefits must be quantified to demonstrate that they outweigh the costs incurred by the implementation of improved cybersecurity measures. There are no sound metrics to indicate how secure a system is, so one cannot articulate how much more secure it would be with additional investment. There is no scientific basis for cost risk analysis, and business decisions are often based on anecdotes or un-quantified arguments of goodness. Currently, it is also very difficult to collect the large body of data needed to develop a good statistical understanding of cyberspace without compromising the privacy of individuals or the reputation of companies. The means to identify and re-align cyber economic incentives and to provide a science-based understanding of markets, decision making, and motivators must be investigated.

Research is required to:

- Explore models of cybersecurity investment and markets
- Develop data models, ontologies, and automatic means of sanitizing data or making data anonymous
- Define meaningful cybersecurity metrics and actuarial tables
- Improve the economic viability of assured software development methods; provide methods to support personal data ownership
- Provide knowledge in support of laws, regulations, and international agreements

3.2. Developing Scientific Foundations

Cyber systems that inspire trust and confidence, protect the privacy and integrity of data resources, and perform reliably are of great importance to society. In anticipation of the challenges in securing the cyber systems of the future, we must develop an organized, cohesive foundation to the body of knowledge that informs the field of cybersecurity. That is the subject of the second thrust of this strategic plan.

Currently, we spend considerable intellectual energy on a patchwork of targeted, tactical activities, some of which lead to significant breakthroughs while others result in a seemingly endless chase to remedy individual vulnerabilities with solutions of limited scope. A more fruitful way to ground research efforts, and to nurture and sustain progress in the kinds of improved cybersecurity solutions that benefit society, is to develop a science of security. Developing a strong, rigorous scientific foundation to cybersecurity helps the field in the following ways:

- *Organizes disparate areas of knowledge* – Provides structure and organization to a broad-based body of knowledge in the form of testable models and predictions
- *Enables discovery of universal laws* – Produces laws that express an understanding of basic, universal dynamics against which to test problems and formulate explanations
- *Applies the rigor of the scientific method* – Approaches problems using a systematic methodology and discipline to formulate hypotheses, design and execute repeatable experiments, and collect and analyze data

The science of security has the potential of producing universal laws that are predictive and transcend specific systems, attacks, and defenses. Within ten years, our aim is to develop a body of laws that apply to real-world settings and provide explanatory value. With these laws, we anticipate being able to reason about classes of entities and develop rubrics that channel research activities into more productive paths.

The scientific approach can facilitate the development of constructs that enable us to draw general conclusions or develop solutions that work for a class of problems. The scientific approach may prove or disprove laws that provide the scientific bases for engineered cybersecurity solutions, or validate or invalidate laws through experimentation. For example, we may posit a law that states that a dynamic defense increases the differential cost of attack. Experiments may validate or invalidate such a law.

The science of security will draw on a range of scientific methods. It is not limited to the traditional, formal mathematical model of reasoning, but extends to experimental science, simulation and data exploration, field studies, social and behavioral science, and principles of engineering. Many scientific investigations in security can benefit from a hypothesis-driven analytic approach with well-designed experiments. Employing common terminology will foster shared frames of reference to enable clear and precise communications. In support of this type of science, we must consider the means to provide shared data sets, agreed-upon test methods, and readily available test facilities. These capabilities can help provide repeatability, robust scientific discourse, grounding for research decisions, and the ability to guide new research efforts.

As we move the discourse forward to lay the scientific foundation for cybersecurity, we recognize many broad-based considerations for prospective scientific contributions. Initially, we expect the government portfolio portion of the science of security to support activities that investigate fundamental laws and enable repeatable experimentation to increase our understanding of the underlying principles of securing complex networked systems. We expect these activities to be intellectually aggressive and include high-risk, multidisciplinary explorations. In the future, as our understanding matures, we anticipate calling out more specific focus areas for science of security research, such as the science of complexity, network science, experimentation-at-scale, etc.

Research is required to develop:

- Methods to model adversaries
- Techniques for component, policy, and system composition
- A control theory for maintaining security in the presence of partially successful attacks
- Sound methods for integrating humans in the system: usability and security
- Quantifiable, forward-looking security metrics (using formal and stochastic modeling methods)
- Measurement methodologies and testbeds for security properties
- Comprehensive, open, and anonymized data repositories

3.3. Maximizing Research Impact

President Obama said in May 2009, "America's economic prosperity in the 21st century will depend on cybersecurity." This pronouncement has ignited a national-level focus on cybersecurity and the need to maximize the impact of R&D on our cybersecurity posture.

Supporting National Priorities

The cybersecurity research themes described in this plan provide a framework within which Federal R&D agencies can address the cybersecurity R&D requirements associated with our national priorities. For example, key cybersecurity challenges in the healthcare, energy, financial services, and defense sectors can be confronted by focusing R&D activities within the framework of the themes. In addition, Federal agencies can leverage the research themes to resolve problems related to establishing and ensuring trusted identities in cyberspace, and to bolster cybersecurity education and training for all cyber-active citizens. The following examples of programs and initiatives highlight the influence of the outlined research themes on national priority areas:

- *Health IT*—The Department of Health and Human Services (HHS), through the Strategic Health IT Advanced Research Projects (SHARP) Program, is developing security and risk mitigation policies and the technologies necessary to build and preserve the public trust as health IT systems gain widespread use.
- *Smart Grid*—The National Institute of Standards and Technology (NIST) recently released guidelines for Smart Grid cybersecurity (NISTIR 7226) that leverage cybersecurity research themes.
- *Financial Services*—The Department of Homeland Security's Directorate for Science and Technology (DHS S&T), NIST, and the Financial Services Sector Coordinating Council (FSSCC) signed an agreement forming a partnership for cybersecurity innovation.
- *National Defense*—Building on research associated with the Deep Understanding of Cyberspace focus area of the Moving Target theme, the Department of Defense is able to develop approaches to the monitoring and attribution of perpetrators of cyber attacks.
- *Transportation*—The Department of Transportation, in conjunction with several other agencies and industry, is sponsoring research to

develop an understanding of cybersecurity and system reliability in surface vehicles, aircraft, and other modes of transportation, and to support wireless infrastructure and applications for surface and air transportation.

- *Trusted Identities*—The National Strategy for Trusted Identities in Cyberspace (NSTIC) articulates the priority to develop an identity ecosystem where individuals and organizations utilize secure, efficient, easy-to-use, and interoperable identity solutions to access online services in a manner that promotes confidence, privacy, choice, and innovation. R&D that is focused on privacy-enhancing technologies, Tailored Trustworthy Spaces, usability, and Cyber Economic Incentives will help shape the identity ecosystem necessary to support Trusted Identities. NITRD is designated as the single lead within the Federal government for research relevant to NSTIC.
- *Cybersecurity Education*—The National Initiative for Cybersecurity Education (NICE) aims to enhance the overall cybersecurity posture of the United States by accelerating the availability of educational and training resources designed to improve the cyber behavior, skills, and knowledge of every segment of the population, enabling a safer cyberspace for all.

Research efforts that align with this strategic plan will address the characteristics that are essential to the desired end states or identify the improvements required to meet these key objectives.

Engaging the Cybersecurity Research Community

An important effect of this strategic plan is that it provides a basis for discussion among researchers aligned to common objectives. The plan includes a component to engage the academic and commercial research communities in stimulating, continuous conversations on cyber threats and on the capabilities required to thwart the threats.

In support of this engagement component, for example, the SCORE IWG is conducting a series of workshops in 2011 to examine the key assumptions that underlie current security architectures. Challenging the key assumptions may open up possibilities for generating novel solutions that reflect a fundamentally different understanding of the problem. Examining key assumptions may also result in validating well-founded assumptions, thereby providing an even stronger basis for moving forward on them. The workshop series focuses on the assumptions that "Defense in Depth is a Smart

Investment," "Trust Anchors are Invulnerable," "Distributed Data Schemes Provide Security," and "Abnormal Behavior Detection Finds Malicious Actors."

In 2011, the NITRD Senior Steering Group for Cybersecurity R&D is sponsoring a workshop to bring together experts to focus on Tailored Trustworthy Spaces. Multiple sectors, such as Smart Grid or Health IT, have a requirement for customizable, private, and secure environments in which to share information and conduct transactions. In the TTS workshop, participants will develop key use cases, identify capabilities needed to address use cases in these sectors, define pilot projects, and inform Federal R&D. Development of technologies and systems that provide the means to establish trusted cyber-subspaces for authorized and appropriate participants and transactions holds the promise of improving the delivery of services in the healthcare, Smart Grid, and financial services sectors.

In addition, individual agencies will continue to engage the research community through solicitations and grants, providing opportunities to support the strategic thrusts directly via the agencies' portfolios. For example, the 2010 Defense Advanced Research Projects Agency (DARPA) Clean-Slate Design of Resilient, Adaptive, Secure Hosts (CRASH) Broad Agency Announcement (BAA) provides research funding for biologically inspired cyber-attack resilience, an element of the Moving Target theme. The 2011 DHS S&T Cyber Security Research and Development BAA provides funding to all the strategic research themes.

In the research community, we intend to make use of multiple avenues and opportunities for engagement. This includes using virtual organizations to promote interaction among disciplines, across sectors, and between the theme areas to pursue progress in cybersecurity. We intend to provide more opportunities for coordination across Federal agencies and with the private sector through mechanisms such as the NITRD program. We expect to put greater focus on the implementation of the research infrastructure that emerges from work on Tailored Trustworthy Spaces, Moving Target, Cyber Economic Incentives, and Designed-in Security. The goal is to enable further research on the effectiveness, viability, and interdependencies of these concepts and technologies. We envision progress by facilitating the early deployment and testing of game-changing cybersecurity prototypes and approaches in advanced computing environments and leading edge IT services.

Although our national-level initiatives focus on research activities within the United States, cyberspace—with its vast interaction space of information, markets, and services—knows no borders. Today's cyberspace facilitates underground economies that violate trust and trade in illicit information. Cyberspace enables misuse as easily as it enables legitimate economic growth. Sharing and cooperation across borders by researchers, governments, and industry are necessary to respond to the rise of global malware pandemics and the common threats they pose. Because the scope of cyberspace is global, we plan to promote this strategic plan at targeted international forums and use existing governmentto-government science and technology mechanisms to begin influencing the focus of international researchers. For example, the INCO-TRUST workshops that are co-organized by the National Science Foundation, the European Commission, and academic institutions represent an international forum at which to engage in discussions of this plan's research themes.

3.4. Accelerating Transition to Practice

An explicit, coordinated process that transitions the fruits of research into practice is essential if Federal cybersecurity R&D investments are to have significant, long-lasting impact. Each research program should have a transition plan that maps the appropriate paths to take a research product into commercialization. Experience shows that the transition plans that a research program develops and executes early in the program's life cycle are the most effective in achieving successful transfer from research to application and use. Transition plans are subject to change and require periodic review and adjustment. Moreover, different technologies are better suited to different technology transition paths. In many instances, the choice of a transition path may ultimately determine the success or failure of the research product in becoming a useful product.

An effective transition plan identifies coordination activities that help manage the transfer of the research component from point to point. Currently, a chasm exists between the research community, which focuses on exercising research components in demonstration environments, and the operations community, which acquires system prototypes containing research components and implements them in operational environments. Bridging that chasm, commonly referred to as the "valley of death," requires cooperative efforts and investments by both the R&D and operations communities, and may involve significant risk-taking on the part of the private sector as it shepherds research results through the commercialization process.

There are a number of transition paths for research funded by the Federal government. These transition paths are affected by the nature of the technology, the intended end-user, participants in the research program, and other external circumstances. Success in research product transition often reflects the dedication of a program manager who works through opportunistic channels of demonstration, partnering, and sometimes good fortune. The most effective approach, however, is to energize a proactive technology champion with the latitude and resources to pursue potential avenues for utilizing the research product. In support of a more systematic and coordinated approach to transition activities, plans can identify resources to reward those who proactively coordinate activities, take risks, and actively engage in the work that transitions a research result successfully into practice.

As part of the Accelerating Transition to Practice activities, the Federal cybersecurity research community plans to participate in the following activities related to technology discovery; test and evaluation; and transition, adoption, and commercialization.

Technology Discovery

NITRD agencies plan to continue existing cross-agency activities and initiate new activities to discover those technologies that are ready for transition. Following are examples of currently planned activities:

- Information Technology Security Entrepreneurs' Forum (ITSEF)
- Principal Investigator (PI) Meetings
- National Labs Technology Expo
- Defense Venture Catalyst Initiative (DeVenCI)

Test and Evaluation

Test and Evaluation (T&E) is an important stage in the successful transition of an innovation from research to deployment and use. T&E requires third-party or partner involvement that focuses experimental deployment efforts on early-stage testing and integration in near-real environments. In this sense, T&E can also be considered an important phase of transition and adoption. NITRD agencies plan to leverage available operational and next-generation networked environments to support experimental deployment, test, and evaluation in realistic settings in both public- and private-sector environments.

Transition, Adoption, and Commercialization

NITRD agencies plan to continue some existing cross-agency activities and initiate other new activities to develop partnerships for those technologies that are ready for transition, adoption, and commercialization. Following are examples of currently planned activities:

- System Integrator Forum (SIF): An open forum for venture capitalists, system integrators, and government managers to review mature R&D products that are being commercialized
- Small Business Innovative Research (SBIR) Conferences: An open forum to showcase cybersecurity SBIR-related research, technology, and products and provide networking opportunities for government customers, Phase II SBIR contractors, and prime contractors

In order to achieve the necessary deployment of new innovation, technology transition must be a key consideration for all R&D investments. R&D processes must allocate and spend program funds on technology transition activities in order to transform the "innovation landscape." R&D programs should plan for later-stage activities that can bridge the transition chasm. In addition, government-funded R&D programs should consider how to best reward government program managers and principal investigators for making measurable progress in this area.

4. Executing the Federal Cybersecurity Research Program

As described in Section 3, the strategy defining the Federal Cybersecurity Research Program is characterized by four primary thrusts: *Inducing Change*—eliminating known cybersecurity deficiencies, *Developing Scientific Foundations*—minimizing future cybersecurity problems, *Maximizing Research Impact*—catalyzing coordination, collaboration, and integration of research activities for maximum effectiveness, and *Accelerating Transition to Practice*—expediting improvements in cyberspace from research findings.

The execution of the Federal Cybersecurity Research Program is vested in several existing government entities with responsibilities for research policies and budgets, coordination, and execution.

4.1. Research Policies

Across the Federal research enterprise, the White House Office of Science and Technology Policy (OSTP) is responsible for leading interagency efforts to develop and implement sound science and technology policies. The mission of OSTP is threefold; first, to provide the President and his senior staff with accurate, relevant, and timely scientific and technical advice on all matters of consequence; second, to ensure that the policies of the Executive Branch are informed by sound science; and third, to ensure that the scientific and technical work of the Executive Branch is properly coordinated so as to provide the greatest benefit to society (see: http://www.whitehouse.gov/ostp).

In the context of the Federal Cybersecurity Research Program, OSTP provides leadership in assuring that strategic research objectives advance national and Presidential priorities and important cybersecurity initiatives are given appropriate visibility.

4.2. Research Coordination

Since its inception in 1991, the Federal Networking and Information Technology Research and Development (NITRD) Program has become the focal point for coordinating interagency research activities in a number of networking and IT domains. Today, the NITRD Program represents a model collaborative enterprise of many Federal agencies in networking, computing, software, cybersecurity, and related information technologies. The NITRD Program is represented through its subcommittee in the National Science and Technology Council.

The NITRD agencies work together in eight major research areas—called Program Component Areas (PCAs). In each PCA, agency program managers participate in an Interagency Working Group (IWG) or Coordinating Group (CG) that coordinates multiagency R&D efforts; budget and program planning; conferences, workshops, and seminars; technical reports and white papers; and preparation of the annual Supplement to the President's Budget for the NITRD Program. Cybersecurity research efforts are coordinated among the agencies in the Cyber Security and Information Assurance IWG. In tandem, the Special Cyber Operations Research and Engineering (SCORE) IWG coordinates research activities related to national security systems. The interagency coordination efforts by both the SCORE IWG and CSIA IWG are augmented and guided by the NITRD Senior Steering Group (SSG) for

Cybersecurity R&D. The Cybersecurity SSG comprises senior agency representatives who have program and budget responsibilities as well as have the authority to establish priorities for their respective organizations. See Figure 1 below.

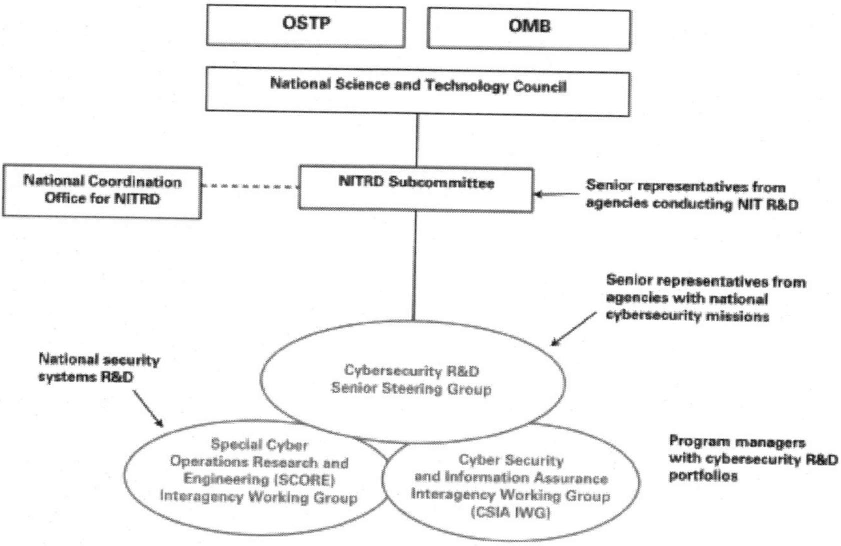

Figure 1. NITRD Structure for Cybersecurity R&D Coordination.

4.3. Research Execution

The coordinated R&D activities are carried out by a group of agencies with varying missions but complementary roles. The primary execution agencies are (in alphabetical order): DARPA, DHS S&T, DoE, IARPA, NIST, NSA, NSF, and OSD and DoD Service research organizations. Among these agencies, the full spectrum of R&D approaches is represented, for example, academic research supported by NSF, applied research supported by DHS, and disruptive technology development by DARPA. Accordingly, each agency structures the contributing R&D activities based on its focus and mission. Highlights of agency activities and research budgets are available from NITRD Supplements to the President's Budget.

ACKNOWLEDGMENTS

This report was developed by the Cyber Security and Information Assurance Research and Development Senior Steering Group (CSIA R&D SSG) and Cyber Security and Information Assurance Interagency Working Group (CSIA IWG). Additional representatives from agencies with cybersecurity R&D programs participated in reviewing the Plan and made technical and editorial contributions to this document. The CSIA R&D SSG and CSIA IWG report to the Subcommittee on Networking and Information Technology Research and Development (NITRD) of the Committee on Technology of the National Science and Technology Council. The report is published by the National Coordination Office for the NITRD Program. For more information, visit http://www.nitrd.gov/.

The contributions of Susan Alexander (National Security Agency), Chris Greer (National Institute of Standards and Technology), and Jeannette Wing (Carnegie Mellon University, on appointment at the National Science Foundation during 2007-2010) are gratefully acknowledged.

ACRONYMS

BAA	Broad Agency Announcement
CRASH	Clean-Slate Design of Resilient, Adaptive, Secure Hosts
CSIA	Cyber Security and Information Assurance
DARPA	Defense Advanced Research Projects Agency
DeVenCI	DoD Venture Catalyst Initiative
DIS	Designed-in Security
DHS S&T	Department of Homeland Security, Directorate for Science and Technology
DoD	Department of Defense
DoE	Department of Energy
FSSCC	Financial Services Sector Coordinating Council
HHS	Department of Health and Human Services
IARPA	Intelligence Advanced Research Projects Agency
ITSEF	Information Technology Security Entrepreneurs' Forum
IWG	Interagency Working Group
MT	Moving Target
NCO	National Coordination Office

NICE	National Initiative for Cybersecurity Education
NITRD	Networking and Information Technology Research and Development
NIST	National Institute of Standards and Technology
NSA	National Security Agency
NSF	National Science Foundation
NSTC	National Science and Technology Council
NSTIC	National Strategy for Trusted Identities in Cyberspace
OMB	Office of Management and Budget
OSD	Office of the Secretary of Defense
OSTP	Office of Science and Technology Policy
PCA	Program Component Area
PI	Principal Investigator
R&D	Research and Development
SBIR	Small Business Innovative Research
SCORE	Special Cyber Operations Research and Engineering
SHARP	Strategic Health IT Advanced Research Projects
SIF	System Integrator Forum
SSG	Senior Steering Group
T&E	Test and Evaluation
TTS	Tailored Trustworthy Space

REFERENCES

Background information and details of the research themes can be found at: http://cybersecurity.nitrd.gov.

End Notes

[1] See http://www.whitehouse.gov/cyberreview/.

[2] For further analysis, see "Cyberspace Policy Review: Assuring a Trusted and Resilient Information and Communications Infrastructure," http://www.whitehouse.gov/assets/documents/Cyberspace_Policy_Review_final.pdf.

[3] For further data on the size and nature of threats, see, for example, "Fiscal Year 2010 Report to Congress on the Implementation of The Federal Information Security Management Act of 2002," http://www.whitehouse.gov/sites/default/files/omb/assets/egov_docs/FY10_FISMA.pdf.

[3] For further data on the size and nature of threats, see, for example, "Fiscal Year 2010 Report to Congress on the Implementation of The Federal Information Security Management Act of 2002," http://www.whitehouse.gov/sites/default/files/omb/assets/egov_docs/FY10_FISMA.pdf.

[4] The National Cyber Leap Year summit was held in 2009. The summit gathered innovators from the academic and commercial sectors for an unconventional exploration of five fundamentally game-changing concepts in cybersecurity. For more information, see http://cybersecurity.nitrd.gov.

[5] For further information, see, for example, "Build Security In," a software assurance strategic initiative of the National Cyber Security Division at the U.S. Department of Homeland Security, https://buildsecurityin.us-cert.gov/bsi/home.html.

In: Federal Cybersecurity
Editor: Cory Medina

ISBN: 978-1-63485-395-8

Chapter 3

REPORT ON IMPLEMENTING THE FEDERAL CYBERSECURITY RESEARCH AND DEVELOPMENT STRATEGY*

Networking and Information Technology Research and Development Program

June 9, 2014

Dear Colleagues:

Today our Nation's security, economic progress, and modern lifestyle all rely upon maintaining a trustworthy digital infrastructure that is resilient and responsive to threats. Critical life-sustaining infrastructures—such as the ones that deliver electricity and water, control air traffic, and support our financial system—all depend on networked information systems making up the Nation's cyberinfrastructure. Information and communication capabilities and technologies have become indispensable to Federal agencies to fulfill their mission responsibilities, but securing these complex and ever-evolving systems poses a formidable technical challenge. After an intensive and deliberate process involving many interactions among the government,

---

* This is an edited, reformatted and augmented version of a document issued by the Networking and Information Technology Research and Development Program, June 2014. Input was provided by the Cyber Security and Information Assurance Research and Development Senior Steering Group (CSIA R&D SSG) and the Cyber Security and Information Assurance Interagency Working Group (CSIA IWG).

industry, and academia, in December 2011 the National Science and Technology Council (NSTC) released *Trustworthy Cyberspace: Strategic Plan for the Federal Cybersecurity Research and Development Program*, a framework for a set of coordinated Federal strategic priorities and objectives for cybersecurity research.

This report, *Report on Implementing the Federal Cybersecurity Research and Development Strategy*, was developed by the National Coordination Office for the Federal Networking and Information Technology Research and Development (NITRD) Program with input from the agencies participating in NITRD on their activities supporting the objectives outlined in the Strategic Plan. The review also considers the public comments on the Strategic Plan that the government solicited. Finally, this report outlines additional technologies and research areas that need further emphasis for the future version of the Strategic Plan.

We are pleased to commend the vigorous response by NITRD agencies to the Federal Cybersecurity R&D Strategic Plan. The findings in this report represent a comprehensive, coordinated, and collaborative effort to secure the Nation's critical cyberinfrastructure. We look forward to continuing this important work with agencies in the coming months as we manage and respond to current and new cybersecurity priorities, and as we prepare for future updates to the Federal Cybersecurity R&D Strategic Plan.

Sincerely,

Farnam Jahanian
NSF Assistant Director, Computer and Information
Science and Engineering Directorate, National Science Foundation
Co-Chair, Subcommittee on Networking and
Information Technology Research and Development

George O. Strawn
Director, National Coordination Office for NITRD
Co-Chair, Subcommittee on Networking and Information
Technology Research and Development

PREFACE

Improving the security and safety of cyberspace—the interconnected information infrastructure of telecommunications networks and computer systems—has been an important priority of President Obama's Administration. Beginning with the *Cyberspace Policy Review: Assuring a Trusted and Resilient Information and Communications Infrastructure,*[1] the President mandated and launched a full spectrum of activities to eliminate or reduce cyberspace vulnerabilities and risks to the Nation's economic and social prosperity. In addition, the President challenged Federal agencies to develop a framework for game-changing cybersecurity research with the goal of fundamentally improving the security, safety, and trustworthiness of the Nation's digital infrastructure.

In December 2011 the National Science and Technology Council (NSTC) released *Trustworthy Cyberspace: Strategic Plan for the Federal Cybersecurity Research and Development Program,*[2] a framework for a set of coordinated Federal strategic priorities and objectives for cybersecurity research. The Strategic Plan was the result of a continuing dialogue between Federal agencies conducting cybersecurity research, agencies with cybersecurity as a critical facet of their mission, and leading industry and academic experts.

The 2011 Strategic Plan was the culmination of many efforts within the Federal Government, spearheaded by the Office of Science and Technology Policy (OSTP) and the Federal Networking and Information Technology Research and Development (NITRD) Program.[3] Three interagency forums coordinated the content of the report: the Cyber Security and Information Assurance Interagency Working Group (CSIA IWG), the Special Cyber Operations Research and Engineering (SCORE) IWG, and the Cyber Security and Information Assurance Research and Development Senior Steering Group (CSIA R&D SSG). Collectively, these groups represent efforts by the primary agencies conducting unclassified cybersecurity research within the Federal Government, including: the Defense Advanced Research Projects Agency (DARPA), Department of Energy (DOE), Department of Homeland Security (DHS), Intelligence Advanced Research Projects Activity (IARPA), National Institute of Standards and Technology (NIST), National Security Agency (NSA), National Science Foundation (NSF), Office of the Secretary of Defense (OSD), and Department of Defense Service research organizations in the Air Force, Army, and Navy.

Federal agencies have initiated and refined an ensemble of new and continuing prioritized research programs to address the challenges identified in the Strategic Plan. In addition to outlining agency strategies for addressing the goals of the Plan and summarizing key efforts directed at the principal research objectives, this report also presents potential areas in which further focus and support would be beneficial.

The four thrusts of the Strategic Plan and their corresponding areas of scientific research should not be taken as the whole of Federal activities in the area of cybersecurity. In fulfilling their mission goals, NITRD agencies have and will continue to engage in a diverse set of supplemental cybersecurity R&D activities on topics not directly addressed in the Strategic Plan or covered in this document. Many of these activities may be critical for the secure functioning of cyber systems of specific interest to agencies, but may not fall into the purview of the harmonized set of current priorities for the Federal cybersecurity R&D enterprise. Specifically, it is important to note that the unclassified research activities outlined are only one portion of the work of the Federal cybersecurity R&D enterprise, of which classified activities are an important additional component.

In February 2013, the President issued Executive Order 13636 (EO 13636), "Improving Critical Infrastructure Cybersecurity,"[4] and Presidential Policy Directive 21 (PPD-21), "Critical Infrastructure Security and Resilience."[5] Executive Order 13636 states "the cyber threat to critical infrastructure continues to grow and represents one of the most serious national security challenges we must confront. The national and economic security of the United States depends on the reliable functioning of the Nation's critical infrastructure in the face of such threats. It is the policy of the United States to enhance the security and resilience of the Nation's critical infrastructure and to maintain a cyberenvironment that encourages efficiency, innovation, and economic prosperity while promoting safety, security, business confidentiality, privacy, and civil liberties."

Within these two documents, the President has specified a new roadmap of activities and goals that the Federal Government must undertake to ensure the cybersecurity of the Nation's critical infrastructure, outlining a plan of policy coordination, information sharing, privacy and civil liberties protection, and the development of frameworks to identify and address cybersecurity risks. Presidential Policy Directive 21 explicitly outlines the roles and responsibilities for different agencies within this directive, including for cybersecurity R&D, specifically:

1) Promoting R&D to enable the secure and resilient design and construction of critical infrastructure and accompanying cyber technology;
2) Enhancing modeling capabilities for determining potential impacts of incident or threat scenarios on critical infrastructure, as well as cascading effects on other sectors;
3) Facilitating initiatives to incentivize cybersecurity investments and the adoption of critical infrastructure design features that strengthen all-hazards security and resilience; and
4) Prioritizing efforts to support the strategic guidance issued by the Secretary of Homeland Security.

The first three goals in PPD-21 are already areas of focus within the Strategic Plan, or outlined as a prospective future priority area within this report. The last goal will require renewed interagency dialogue and coordination to synchronize the Secretary of Homeland Security's efforts with the extensive and ongoing Federal cybersecurity R&D enterprise outlined in this document.

As the NITRD CSIA IWG co-chairs, we are gratified by the exceptional level of cybersecurity research coordination that the Strategic Plan has initiated, and we are confident that a continuing focus on the objectives of this Plan and its coordination by NITRD groups will contribute significantly to securing cyberspace.

Douglas Maughan, DHS S&T
William Newhouse, NIST

Co-Chairs
NITRD Cyber Security and Information Assurance Interagency Working Group (CSIA IWG)

1. INTRODUCTION

The Nation's security, economic progress, and modern lifestyle are increasingly dependent on cyberinfrastructure—the vast, interconnected information networks, communications technologies, and computer systems that handle the processing and flow of information across the many distributed environments and resources of cyberspace. This increasing reliance must be matched with assurances that information and communication technologies can securely support the core activities underpinning cyberspace. However, the history of the creation of the Internet has left a legacy in its structure and design that makes securing cyberinfrastructure today a massive technical challenge. The Internet was originally developed to support a new mode of communication and information sharing between scientists at different institutions. Since all the users were members of a relatively small and exclusive group, flexibility and scalability, not security, were the key attributes of its design. While these attributes have enabled the innovations that have driven rapid growth and adoption of the technology, the community of Internet users is no longer a small and friendly club, but rather a global ecosystem of interconnected players with diverse needs, capabilities, and motives. It is very difficult now to retrofit trust mechanisms into the Internet and to achieve the level of security required for cyberinfrastructure and the systems dependent on it.

In December 2011 the NSTC released *Trustworthy Cyberspace: Strategic Plan for the Federal Cybersecurity Research and Development Program*, outlining a vision for the research needed to develop game-changing technologies to neutralize attacks on the cyber systems of today, and to establish scientific foundations to meet the challenges of securing the cyber systems of tomorrow. The Strategic Plan surfaced intersections of common interest and mutual benefit in cybersecurity research; outlined specific research and development areas that span multiple disciplines; and emphasized collaboration among researchers and technical experts in government, industry, academia, and international contexts.

Since the release of the Strategic Plan, Federal agencies have responded vigorously by adapting their existing cybersecurity R&D programs and initiating new activities that align with the Plan's strategic priorities. This report summarizes the broad Federal response, highlighting the specific research activities that agencies are supporting. This report finds that, since the release of the Strategic Plan, agencies have coordinated successfully to minimize duplication among R&D efforts and made excellent progress in creating and leveraging partnerships with other agencies and external parties on key research areas. Agencies have also put proper focus on transitioning research to practice and maximizing the impact of their R&D investments.

Looking forward to the near future, the framework outlined in the Strategic Plan remains pertinent and viable; the four strategic thrusts of **Inducing Change**, **Developing Scientific Foundations**, **Maximizing Impact**, and **Accelerating Transition to Practice** are still the key areas of Federal action needed to help create a cyber-safe Nation. However, given recent advancements in technology, new needs, and an improved understanding of the foundations of cybersecurity, additional areas within each thrust have emerged that require emphasis. Some of these areas of emphasis are discussed in this document. In addition, two broader areas for cybersecurity research have emerged as critical to the function of our Nation and to the fulfillment of agency mission goals: **Privacy and Protected Disclosure** and the **Security of Cyber-Physical Systems**. Though both can be considered facets of the research themes within the 2011 Strategic Plan, they have risen in importance and warrant explicit highlighting as priority research areas.

As the emergence of new technologies and capabilities drives increasing dependency on cyberinfrastructure, the Federal Government must match the growth in information and communication technology with an expanded investment in cybersecurity R&D. Research into the newly identified priority research areas outlined in this document must be conducted in tandem with ongoing activities. Reflecting this need for more investment, the President's FY 2015 budget request proposes $715 million for unclassified cybersecurity R&D activities through the NITRD agencies – an increase of $62 million over the $653 million in actual expenditures for FY 2013.[6]

2. Overview and Scope

This report on the implementation of the Federal cybersecurity R&D strategy follows the basic outline of the 2011 Strategic Plan, organizing topical areas into four strategic thrusts and, within each thrust, into key research themes and focus areas. The report covers two main areas: a summary of R&D activities at each of the primary NITRD agencies (Sections 4-5) and an analysis of the Federal response and proposals for next steps (Sections 6-7). Section 3 restates the framework of four strategic thrusts articulated in the Plan, establishing the context for the subsequent sections. Section 4 provides an overview of agency responses to the Strategic Plan and identifies the relationship of the responses to the four strategic thrusts. Section 5 gives an overview of the types of activities pursued within each of the thrusts and highlights specific examples of relevant programs and projects. Section 6 analyzes the accomplishments, gaps, and overlaps in the Federal response to the 2011 Plan, and identifies emerging areas where additional emphasis may be warranted. Section 7 outlines next steps to be taken by NITRD in continuing the dialogue, both within the Federal Government and externally, to address the Strategic Plan.

As part of this review, public comments[7] on the Strategic Plan were solicited to gain insights from experts in industry, academia, and the public. These comments enhance understanding of the research and implementation challenges of the Strategic Plan, and continue the open dialogue that is needed between the government and the technical community at-large to help refine and improve the Plan. Key comments and responses are noted within the pertinent sections of this document, as applicable.

In addition to discussing the topics presented in the Strategic Plan, the public comments stressed the importance of policy, education, usability, funding, transparency, and accountability as critical aspects of a responsive national cybersecurity enterprise. Although these topics are outside the scope of an R&D-focused Strategic Plan, it is worth noting that many agencies have programs that target some of these areas; for example, NSF is funding two research centers around the social, behavioral, and economic perspectives of cybersecurity.[8] Within this broader social and technological context for cybersecurity, the NITRD Program identified "Cyber Economic Incentives" as a high-impact priority and explicitly targeted research in this area. In the future, as other topics move toward the forefront and become key enablers or barriers to maintaining a secure cyberspace, NITRD agencies and the Administration are prepared to respond with additional R&D focused on those topics.

Finally, it is important to note that this document outlines only the research activities conducted by the Federal Government in the unclassified domain. Scoping of unclassified research priorities is part of a greater research context that includes U.S. Government-funded classified R&D activities, ongoing domestic private sector research, and international cybersecurity research and development activities.

3. Summary of the Federal Cybersecurity R&D Strategy

The Strategic Plan provides a framework of four strategic thrusts to organize activities and drive progress in cybersecurity R&D:

- **Inducing Change** – Utilizing game-changing themes to direct efforts towards understanding the underlying root causes of known current threats with the goal of disrupting the status quo with radically different approaches to improve the security of the critical cyber systems and infrastructure that serve society.
- **Developing Scientific Foundations** – Developing an organized, cohesive scientific foundation to the body of knowledge that informs the field of cybersecurity through adoption of a systematic, rigorous, and disciplined scientific approach. Promoting the discovery of laws, hypothesis testing, repeatable experimental designs, standardized data-gathering methods, metrics, common terminology, and critical analysis that engenders reproducible results and rationally based conclusions.
- **Maximizing Research Impact** – Catalyzing integration across the game-changing R&D themes, cooperation between governmental and private-sector communities, collaboration across international borders, and strengthening linkages to other national priorities, such as health IT and Smart Grid.
- **Accelerating Transition to Practice** – Focusing efforts to ensure adoption and implementation of the powerful new technologies and strategies that emerge from the research themes, and the activities to build a scientific foundation so as to create measurable improvements in the cybersecurity landscape.

4. Agency Missions Aligned with the Federal Cybersecurity R&D Strategy

The Strategic Plan identifies high priority cyber capabilities that hold promise for enabling fundamental improvements in the security and trustworthiness of cyberspace. To achieve these capabilities, the Plan defines an R&D framework that organizes objectives and activities across a range of R&D efforts, including those that require coordination across multiple agencies and those that an individual agency might support in the context of its particular mission, capabilities, and expertise. For example, NSF, which serves to promote the progress of science, contributes to the Plan's objectives by funding academic research on the scientific foundations of security. DARPA, which aims to maintain the technological superiority of the U.S. military, contributes to the Plan's objectives by sponsoring the development of revolutionary, high-payoff defense technologies to maximize research impact.

Collectively, the agencies execute a coordinated portfolio of R&D activities from basic science to mission-specific capabilities. No single agency addresses all the priority areas in the Strategic Plan nor should it. Instead, it is the many different agency efforts comprising the Federal cybersecurity R&D enterprise that, with guidance from the Strategic Plan and coordination through NITRD, enables progress towards the Plan's goals. This section summarizes the unique aspects of agency research strategies for addressing the goals and challenges outlined in the Strategic Plan.

Air Force Research Laboratory (AFRL)

AFRL's efforts in cybersecurity aim to create a firm, trustable foundation in cyberspace, and then to build assured mission capabilities upon it. New technologies are needed to be aware of missions and threats, compute optimal assurance solutions, and implement protection as needed via mission agility or infrastructure reinforcement. The capabilities developed through this research will be more agile and resilient than current solutions, providing the ability to avoid, fight through, survive, and recover from advanced cyber threats. They will also be more effective at engaging and optimizing the role of humans in cyberspace operations.

Army Research Laboratory (ARL)

ARL's mission is to provide the science, technology, and analysis that underpin full-spectrum military operations. Within its mission, ARL contributes to a number of the Strategic Plan's objectives with a particular focus on Moving Target technologies within its **Cyber Maneuver Initiative**. The Cyber Maneuver Initiative aims to improve defense against advanced persistent threats by creating dynamic attack surfaces for protected systems, and includes research in dynamic operating system maneuverability, application diversity, network agility, cyber deception, predictive cyber threat modeling, and cognitive reasoning and feedback to maximize maneuver effectiveness in tactical environments.

Defense Advanced Research Projects Agency (DARPA)

DARPA is the principal agency within the Department of Defense for high-risk, high-payoff research, development, and demonstration of new technologies and systems that serve the warfighter and the Nation's defense. DARPA's R&D efforts in cybersecurity strongly support the Moving Target and Tailored Trustworthy Spaces themes. In particular, DARPA's **Information Assurance and Survivability Program** seeks to draw on biological and immune systems as inspiration for radically re-thinking computer hardware, software, and system designs. Such systems will be able to detect, diagnose, and respond to attacks by employing their own innate and adaptive immune systems. Furthermore, in response to attacks, such systems will also be capable of dynamically adapting and improving their defensive capabilities over time. As in biological systems, the cyber systems will dynamically diversify, increasing their resiliency and survivability, and that of their individual, constituent computers.

Department of Energy (DOE)

A key mission of the DOE Office of Electricity Delivery and Energy Reliability (OE) is to enhance the reliability and resiliency of the Nation's energy infrastructure. Within DOE OE's **Cybersecurity for Energy Delivery Systems (CEDS) Program**, cybersecurity R&D is tailored to the unique performance requirements, designs, and operational environments of energy delivery systems. The CEDS Program operates with the goal that, by 2020, resilient energy delivery systems are designed, installed, operated, and maintained to survive cyber-incidents while sustaining critical functions. To help achieve this vision, OE fosters and actively engages in collaborations among all energy stakeholders – utility, vendor, national lab, and academic. Through these collaborations, OE seeks to solve hand-in-hand with industry the "right problems," and to transition next-generation research from the national labs and academia into commercial products operating in the energy sector. The Strategic Plan research themes, particularly Designed-In Security and Tailored Trustworthy Spaces are strongly supported by the strategies and milestones outlined in the CEDS Program.

Other elements of DOE also perform related cybersecurity research. The Advanced Scientific Computing Research (ASCR) Program, which is part of the Office of Science, sponsors research to support DOE's world leadership in scientific computation. Security of networks and middleware is a critical element in the ASCR Next Generation Networking research program. The National Nuclear Security Administration (NNSA) within DOE also sponsors cybersecurity research to support its unique mission requirements.

Department of Homeland Security (DHS)

The DHS Science and Technology Directorate Cyber Security Division (DHS S&T CSD) focuses on applied research and development, test, evaluation, and transition for technologies to support civilian Federal, state, and local governments and private sector unclassified needs to protect the Nation's cyber infrastructure. Of particular interest to DHS are technologies that can be developed and transitioned to commercial products or used in Federal, state, and local government systems. DHS S&T CSD has promoted innovation and accelerated transition to practice by using Broad Agency Announcements (BAA) to solicit research proposals, supporting the **Small Business Innovation Research (SBIR)** program, participating in and initiating public-private partnerships, and collaborating with Federal agencies and international partners through joint project funding and management. In FY 2011, DHS S&T CSD issued BAA 11-02 which solicited proposals for R&D in 14 technical areas, spanning all research themes of the Strategic Plan.

Intelligence Advanced Research Projects Activity (IARPA)

IARPA's cybersecurity research is spearheaded by its Office of Safe and Secure Operations (SSO), which aims to counter emerging adversary potential to ensure the U.S. Intelligence Community's operational effectiveness in a globally interdependent and networked environment. SSO's research portfolio is organized into three areas: computational power, trustworthy components, and safe and secure systems. Objectives within the computational power area include developing revolutionary advances in science and engineering to solve problems intractable with today's computers, focusing on the fundamental elements of quantum computing systems, and exploring the feasibility of a superconducting computer. In the trustworthy components area, research programs focus on understanding and manipulating very small-scale electronics, obtaining mission-worthy chips from state-of-the-art, but untrusted fabrication facilities, and gaining functionality from un-pedigreed software without placing mission systems at risk. Finally, research in the safe and secure systems area has a broad objective of safeguarding the integrity of missions in a hostile environment. Some of the current projects focus on enabling collaboration without wholesale sharing of data through privacy-preserving search techniques. Research in both the trustworthy components and safe and secure systems areas contributes directly to the Tailored Trustworthy Spaces research theme.

National Institute of Standards and Technology (NIST)

NIST's Information Technology Laboratory (ITL) is a recognized thought leader in cryptography, identity management, key management, mobile security, risk management, security automation, security of networked systems, foundations of measurement science for information systems, secure virtualization, cloud security, trusted roots of hardware, usability and security, and vulnerability management. ITL is comprised of six divisions; each has ongoing work that moves the Nation towards the end-state vision of the Cybersecurity R&D Strategic Plan. In particular, the NIST Software and Systems Division (SSD) works with industry, academia, and other government agencies to increase trust and confidence in deployed software, standards and testing tools for today's software infrastructures and tomorrow's next-generation software systems, and conformance testing. Additionally, the NIST Computer Security Division (CSD) within ITL leads the Government's efforts in risk management, identity management, key management, security automation, mobile security, trusted roots for hardware, vulnerability management, and cryptography. CSD's activities in key management, multi-factor authentication, and identity management strongly contribute to the Tailored Trustworthy Spaces theme. Among its recent priorities, CSD's efforts in information security continuous monitoring support the Moving Target theme—by developing tools and specifications that maintain ongoing awareness of information security, vulnerabilities, and threats to support organizational risk management decisions. The NIST National Cybersecurity Center of Excellence (NCCoE) and National Strategy for Trusted Identities in Cyberspace (NSTIC) Program Management Office are focused on driving adoption of cybersecurity and identity management standards and best practices to support measurable improvements in the cybersecurity landscape.

National Security Agency (NSA)

NSA has several research efforts exploring the Tailored Trustworthy Spaces theme, including exploration of risk through behavioral analytics and large-scale data analysis, novel means to detect modifications to computing systems and network analytics, and efforts to customize system controls. NSA is also exploring Moving Target technologies. By conducting a full scope analysis of the Moving Target problem and solution space, NSA plans to develop "movement" prototypes and evaluate several critical enabling functions. In partnership with the DoD, the agency produced a survey of current Moving Target techniques, thereby enabling a cost-benefit analysis that will take into account different approaches and technologies, the potential impact Moving Target protections may have on mission operations, the costs and overheads associated with implementation, and the overall effectiveness of the movement response. Additionally, NSA is supporting activities that foster an interdisciplinary collaborative community around the science of security, including a virtual organization and four university-based multidisciplinary research centers.

National Science Foundation (NSF)

NSF invests in cybersecurity research through several programs, including the Directorate of Engineering (ENG) programs in Communications, Circuits, and Sensing-Systems (CCSS) and Energy, Power, and Adaptive Systems (EPAS). A major program in cybersecurity is spearheaded by the NSF Directorate of Computer and Information Science and Engineering (CISE), in collaboration with the Directorates of Education and Human Resources (EHR), Engineering (ENG), Mathematical and Physical Sciences (MPS), and Social, Behavioral & Economic Sciences (SBE). NSF's solicitation for the **Secure and Trustworthy Cyberspace (SaTC) Program** provides funding to university investigators for research activities on all four Strategic Plan thrusts, with an explicit option for transition to practice projects. The solicitation provides funding for projects related to cybersecurity education, as well as social, behavioral, and economic perspectives on cybersecurity. Another major program is **CyberCorps: Scholarship for Service (SFS)** led by the EHR Directorate. This program supports cybersecurity education and workforce development. NSF's program is distinguished from other agency efforts by its comprehensive nature, and by the strong role of research on cybersecurity foundations.

Office of Naval Research (ONR)

ONR cybersecurity strategies focus on long- and medium-term scientific and technology areas that have the potential for delivering significant improvements in the robustness, resiliency, security, and operational effectiveness of cyber environments. ONR's cybersecurity research contributes strongly to the objectives identified in the Moving Target, Tailored Trustworthy Spaces, and Designed-In Security areas. The Moving Target theme is particularly supported by the **Robust and Autonomic Computing Systems Program**, a long-term initiative for exploring architectures and approaches for future adaptive computing systems. Research in the Tailored Trustworthy Spaces area is supported by the **Fabric Project** a medium-term project providing strong, principled security guarantees based on explicitly stated security policies, and does so for distributed systems with complex, incomplete, and changing trust between participants. Additional programs such as **Automation in Cryptology, Software Efficiency Reclamation, Computer Network Defense and Information Assurance,** and **Quantum Information Sciences** contribute to the Strategic Plan by developing novel capabilities and technologies across the research themes. At the Georgia Institute of Technology, ONR-funded researchers investigated the theory and models for botnets, and developed state of the art algorithms, methods, and tools for detecting and tracking botnets and their command and control. Their research has been invaluable for the DoD, as well as the tools developed and now in use by the FBI for taking down botnets and tracking down bot-masters and individual operators. Additionally, ONR promotes underexplored research topics that have promising impacts on cybersecurity. For example, at the University of California, ONR is supporting a technical investigation of the underground economy that allows botnets to exist.

Office of the Secretary of Defense (OSD)

DoD's cybersecurity science and technology programs emphasize game-changing research over incremental approaches, and enhance the organizational ties and experimental infrastructure needed to accelerate transition of new technologies into practice. To strengthen its ability to pursue a coordinated set of objectives and a shared vision in cybersecurity, the Assistant Secretary of Defense for Research and Engineering (ASD(R&E)) formed the **DoD Cyber S&T Community of Interest (DoD Cyber COI)**. The DoD has specialized needs in cybersecurity due to the nature of its national security and warfighting mission. The DoD Cyber COI was charged with developing a DoD Cyber S&T problem statement, challenge areas that address warfighter requirements, a research framework, priority technology areas, and, in particular, a Cyber S&T Roadmap of current and needed research in cybersecurity.

The Cyber S&T Roadmap lays out four areas of research: Foundations of Trust, Resilient Infrastructure, Agile Operations, and Assuring Effective Missions. All four areas relate strongly to the Designed-In Security theme, strengthening different attributes of security through development, design, and validation methods, component and system design, algorithms, protocols, and architecture. The Foundations of Trust area contributes particularly to the Tailored Trustworthy Spaces theme. The Resilient Infrastructure and Agile Operations areas support the Moving Target theme. All four Roadmap areas have research challenges that will contribute to the foundational Science of Security.

5. Implementing the Strategic Plan: Agency Highlights and Accomplishments

5.1. Inducing Change

Achieving enduring trustworthiness of cyberspace requires new paradigms that re-balance the security asymmetries of today's cyber environment. The major challenges and new paradigms needed to overcome them motivate R&D agendas in four research themes:

- **Moving Target**: The cost of attacks is asymmetric, favoring the attacker, and so defenders must increase the cost of attack and employ methods that enable them to continue to operate in the face of attack;
- **Tailored Trustworthy Spaces**: The burden of simultaneously satisfying all the requirements of an ideal cybersecurity solution is impossibly high, and so we must enable sub-spaces in cyberspace to

support different security policies and different security services for different types of interactions;

- **Designed-In Security**: The prevalent software design and development methodologies and tools handicap designers' capability to design, develop, and evolve high-assurance systems that are resistant to attacks, and so we must increase our ability to utilize assurance-focused engineering practices that enable reasoning about a diversity of quality attributes (security, safety, reliability, etc.) while providing the evidence necessary to prove the system's resistance to vulnerabilities;
- **Cyber Economic Incentives**: The lack of meaningful metrics and economically sound decision making in security misallocates resources, and so we must promote economic principles in identifying and realigning economic and social incentives that encourage the broad use of good cybersecurity practices and deter illicit activities.

The four research themes provide a shared and unifying set of objectives with the most promising impacts on national cybersecurity issues. Federal cybersecurity research strategies focus on the research themes and on enabling component technologies supportive of, or required by, these themes. However, the themes do not preclude agencies from undertaking other research activities that are necessary to fulfilling their missions. Overlying these challenges is the need for agencies to achieve impactful results in their mission responsibilities balanced with operational costs, scalability, and usability. These additional attributes are critical in enabling the smooth transition to practice of cybersecurity research, which is discussed in further detail in Section 5.4.

5.1.1. Moving Target

The vision and goals of the Moving Target research theme are as follows:

Vision

Develop, evaluate, and deploy diverse mechanisms and strategies that dynamically shift and change over time in order to increase complexity and costs for attackers, limit the exposure of vulnerabilities and opportunities for attack, and increase system resiliency.

Goals

- Design resilient systems that operate reliably in compromised environments
- Increase the cost of staging and executing attacks
- Shift from reactive security postures to active preemptive postures
- Develop Moving Target mechanisms that create disruptions for the adversaries, but not for legitimate users
- Develop the ability to optimize Moving Target mechanisms against various attacks and disruptions

At a high level, the research supported by agencies within the Moving Target theme can be grouped along several contributing characteristics:

- Frameworks
- Techniques
- Scientific foundations

5.1.1.1. Frameworks

A number of research activities include investigating and developing novel frameworks for managing systems that employ Moving Target mechanisms and strategies. For example, DHS, NSF, and DARPA are funding research efforts that use biological concepts—such as those related to immune systems, genetic algorithms, and social insect behaviors—to create distributed cyber systems that are flexible when responding to a cyber-attack. In the same way that biological systems are constantly aware, adapting, and evolving, these systems are designed to detect new anomalous code or attack methods, adapt and repair after a cyber-attack, and cope with new vulnerabilities that can be introduced over time. These "nature-inspired solutions" were called out as a focus area in the Moving Target theme of the Strategic Plan, and many agencies have coalesced around the concept in novel and unique ways.

Spotlight on DARPA –
Clean-Slate Design of Resilient, Adaptive, Secure Hosts (CRASH) and Mission-oriented Resilient Clouds (MRC) Programs

Announced in June 2010, DARPA's **Clean-Slate Design of Resilient, Adaptive, Secure Hosts (CRASH) Program** is focused on designing new and revolutionary architectures that make computer systems highly resistant to cyber-attacks. The objective is to design systems that are able to adapt and continue rendering useful services after a successful attack, learn from previous attacks on how to guard against and cope with future attacks, and repair themselves after attacks have succeeded.

CRASH has initiated projects in three biologically inspired areas: The Innate Immunity area has the goal of eliminating all common technical vulnerabilities, with solutions focused primarily on hardware, operating systems, middleware, and formal methods. The Adaptive Immunity area works in cooperation with Innate components at a higher level in the stack and includes projects to develop techniques for identifying, diagnosing, and recovering from new attacks. The Dynamic Diversity area is inspired by the biological concept of diversity leading to survivability. In this area, techniques are being developed that make each computer different from every other computer, and make each computer differ from itself over time. This raises an attacker's work factor while maintaining system manageability.

One of CRASH's achievements is the Diversity Compiler: compiler technologies that make it possible to create diverse versions of applications and operating systems that behave in exactly the same way under normal use, but do not share vulnerabilities among them. By changing characteristics, such as the specific machine instructions a program uses or the way it is placed into memory, users see no changes in program behavior; attackers, however, are forced to break into each unique instance and are prevented from reusing a single attack across millions of computers. The CRASH Program has also developed a prototype hardware-software system to enforce a number of formal assurance and protection principles. For example, it can restrict access within a host to only what is essential for a given program, following the principle of least privilege.

Building on the successes of CRASH, DARPA's **Mission-oriented Resilient Clouds (MRC) Program** is developing technologies to detect, diagnose, and respond to attacks in cloud computing systems so that cloud applications and infrastructure can continue functioning while under attack. These technologies use cloud resources to relocate computations so that attackers are not able to find them, and to induce artificial diversity across hosts so that no two hosts present the same configuration to the attacker. Additionally, resources can be grouped to provide collective defense, automatically detect and diagnose any system penetration, automatically develop work-arounds and patches, and distribute these solutions around the cloud so that the entire system learns from each individual host. Ultimately, the system as a whole becomes more secure and resilient than any individual host.

Spotlight on ONR –
Robust Autonomic Host Program

ONR's **Robust Autonomic Host Program** is focused on developing computing systems that can self-heal, operate under attack with reduced capabilities, employ artificial diversity to increase resilience, and engage in disinformation as an element of Moving Target defense. Initiated in FY 2011, this program supports exploratory and experimental research towards achieving robust, resilient, and autonomic computing in the future. The program covers wide areas of research and engineering applicable to computing infrastructure, including efficient and adaptive data-acquisition and monitoring, machine intelligence, machine reasoning and strategic planning, automated diagnostics, artificial diversity, and automated strategic deception. An autonomic computing system that continuously assesses its own state, health, capabilities and limitations, and adapts to the situation at cyber speed, can maximize mission success while reducing operational cost.

5.1.1.2. Techniques

A significant portion of Moving Target research involves developing techniques that modify system characteristics in one or more dimensions. For example:

- Policies – risk adaptive policies, movement scheduling
- System of systems – non-persistent virtual machines, system self-cleansing, machine rotations
- Data – secure distributed data chunking and decentralization, data encryption
- Networks – dynamic networking, dynamic Domain Name System (DNS), Internet Protocol (IP) address randomization
- Software – source code diversity, just-in-time compiling, disposable applications
- System – diversity in operating systems, instruction set randomization
- Hardware – multicore processing, cache randomization

At Sandia National Laboratories, both AFRL and DOE have programs to develop technologies that can rapidly change or randomize network addresses and device paths; from an attacker's perspective, this results in a constantly changing and difficult to understand network layout. IARPA is conducting research in software techniques to automate processes for modifying software code to neutralize vulnerabilities. DHS's Moving Target Defense Program focuses on a wide variety of Moving Target techniques within different layers of the hardware and software stack.

Spotlight on AFRL – Cyber Agility Initiative

AFRL has been at the forefront of Moving Target research with initiatives such as the **Cyber Agility Initiative**, announced in FY 2011. This initiative's objective is to make it harder for a determined adversary to succeed by increasing agility, diversity, and redundancy, and by disrupting attack plans and execution.

In FY 2012 AFRL launched the **Polymorphic Machines and Enclaves Program** within the Cyber Agility Initiative. Polymorphic machines use continuously changing computer and system characteristics in a manner that is controlled by the transformation and diversification process, and yet appear to an attacker to be a randomly shifting target space. At the same time, however, the systems maintain transparency and utility for authorized users. The concept of polymorphic machines is extended to the entire network in the Polymorphic Enclaves Program, which aims to create rapidly shifting network architectures with automated agility and diversity mechanisms to modify or morph the network continually, dynamically, and unpredictably into secure operational modes, both before and during attacks.

In addition to these new programs, the Cyber Agility Initiative is responsible for the successful **Active Repositioning in Cyberspace for Synchronized Evasion (ARCSYNE)** technology, which is entering into pilot projects with other agencies. This technology employs IP address hopping to create an agile and stealthy network where the network identity of hosts changes rapidly to confuse attackers. In a one-year follow-up project, started in Q4 of 2012, DHS is funding expansion of the technology to include higher network speeds and network management capabilities. The expected outcome at the end of this project will be a fully functioning network appliance unit that can operate as close to 10 Gbps as possible and change IP addresses in the network at least 10 times/second.

Spotlight on IARPA – Securely Taking On New Executable Software Of Uncertain Provenance (STONESOUP) Program

The IARPA **Securely Taking On New Executable Software Of Uncertain Provenance (STONESOUP) Program** seeks to automate the detection and mitigation of security vulnerabilities in software applications while diversifying program code, so that residual vulnerabilities are harder to exploit. STONESOUP is also investigating novel techniques for randomizing, rewriting, or monitoring software application code so that an adversary will not be able to predict the location of instructions or data needed to launch malicious exploits. The goal of the program is to be able to mitigate security vulnerabilities of software with uncertain provenance automatically without relying on expensive and limited manual security evaluations.

The program began in September 2010 and is slated to end in November 2014. Phase 2 currently has four funded projects developing techniques for sound analysis of software, for automatically inferring reasonable security policies, and for automatically mitigating vulnerabilities without expert human interaction. Phase 1 was successfully completed, demonstrating the ability to neutralize (render unexploitable) over 75% of two types of seeded vulnerabilities in 10,000 line programs while preserving normal program behaviors. Phase 2 goals are to increase the size of programs to 100,000 lines of code, to increase the number of vulnerability types to four, and to demonstrate that 80% of vulnerabilities are automatically mitigated. Future Phase 3 goals include 500,000 line programs, six types of vulnerabilities, and requirements for a 90% rate of vulnerability neutralization with no more than a 10% increase in runtime overhead.

Spotlight on DHS – Moving Target Defense Program

DHS's **Moving Target Defense Program** pursues new capabilities and technologies in several Moving Target areas. These include (1) integration of self-cleaning, intrusion-tolerant servers with reactive systems, (2) active kernel updates that keep system attack surfaces dynamic, (3) IP version 6 (IPv6) integration with IP-address hopping technology, (4) development of obfuscation and virtual instance randomization technologies, (5) binary program randomization, (6) translation of insect colony behavioral models into algorithms for rapidly detecting malware, and (7) applying bio-sequence analysis to discover anomalous sequences of transactions within networks.

The program was initiated under a 2012 DHS BAA which awarded four contracts and five SBIR awards. Current work includes innovative hardware cache designs to increase resiliency, improvements to the ARCSYNE system, novel bio-inspired approaches to intrusion and anomalous behavior detection, a multi-kernel OS architecture that increases system resilience and minimizes the effect of Moving Target Defense on mission-critical tasks, IPhopping utilizing IPv6, and Multi-layer Ever-changing Self-defense Services (MESS) that are both resilient and manageable. The bio-inspired solutions may ultimately change the current approach used for developing intrusion detection systems. New attack methods will quickly be detected rather than relying on the knowledge of existing, known malicious software or cyberattacks.

5.1.1.3. Scientific Foundations of Moving Target

Integral to Moving Target research is a scientific foundation for understanding and analyzing the effectiveness of Moving Target frameworks and mechanisms. These analyses show what classes of attacks are stopped by particular mechanisms, how to compare different approaches, and how to assess the effectiveness of the techniques.

Scientific foundations of Moving Target are the focus of the Army Research Office's (ARO) Moving Target Defense Program, a five-year, multidisciplinary university research project that began in July 2013. The goal of the program is to establish scientific foundations of adaptive systems that are robust, resilient, and survivable against cyber-attacks. In conjunction with the ARO effort, and also beginning in late FY 2013, ARL has established a new collaborative venture—the **Cyber Security Collaborative Research Alliance (CRA)**—that seeks to advance interdisciplinary, theoretical foundations of cyber science in the context of Army networks. NSA is also contributing to the scientific foundations of Moving Target by developing an assessment and taxonomies of techniques and methodologies for their analysis, and by having organized the first National Symposium on Moving Target Research, held in Annapolis, MD in June 2012.[9]

Spotlight on ARL –
Cyber Security
Collaborative Research Alliance (CRA)

ARL has established a new collaborative venture—the **Cyber Security Collaborative Research Alliance**—that seeks to advance the interdisciplinary, theoretical foundations of cyber science in the context of Army networks, focused in part on cyber agility in its inter-relations with theories of cyber detection of malicious activities, characterization of risks, and crosscutting issues of psychosocial aspects in cyber agility. The CRA consists of academia, industry, and government researchers working jointly to solve complex problems. The Agility Research Area seeks to develop theories and models to support planning and control of cyber maneuver (i.e., "maneuver" in the space of network characteristics and topologies) that would describe how control and end-state of the maneuver are influenced by fundamental properties of threats, such as might be rapidly inferred from limited observations of a new, recently observed threat. The Risk Research Area seeks to develop theories and models that relate fundamental properties and features of dynamic risk assessment algorithms to the fundamental properties of dynamic cyber threats, Army's networks, and defensive mechanisms. The Detection Research Area seeks to develop theories and models that relate properties and capabilities of cyber threat detection and recognition processes/mechanisms to properties of a malicious activity, and of properties of Army networks. This research should inform development of approaches to rapid adaptation (potentially in the midst of a battle) of a detection technique or algorithm as new threats emerge. Psychosocial effects will be studied across all three areas; since teams of human defenders will likely be the key link in cyber defense, a theoretical understanding of the socio-cognitive factors that impact the decision making of the user/soldier, defender/analyst, and adversary needs to be developed.

5.1.2. Tailored Trustworthy Spaces

The vision and goals of the Tailored Trustworthy Spaces research theme are as follows:

Vision

- Create flexible and distributed trust environments that can support a range of functional and policy requirements arising from a wide spectrum of activities in cyberspace.
- Support operating capabilities across multiple dimensions, including confidentiality, anonymity, data and system integrity, provenance, availability, and performance.

Goals

- Enable trustworthy computing in untrustworthy environments
- Develop a common framework that supports varying trustworthy space policies and context-specific trust services for different types of actions and transactions
- Develop rules, measurable metrics of trustworthiness, flexible trust negotiation tools, configuration decision support capabilities, and the ability to perform informed trust analysis.

Research in Tailored Trustworthy Spaces can be organized along the following high-level dimensions:

- Characterization
- Trust negotiation
- Operations
- Privacy

5.1.2.1. Characterization

Research in the characterization of Tailored Trustworthy Spaces aims to identify and specify elements that describe the space, translate operational requirements into policies, define tailoring requirements, and translate tailoring requirements into executable rules.

Agency research efforts also support the characterization of specific application areas of Tailored Trustworthy Spaces. For example, NSF is funding researchers at Carnegie Mellon University to investigate the semantics and enforcement of privacy policies, particularly for healthcare. Legal requirements for healthcare records are different from those associated with traditional computer security access in that first, they often include restrictions on future uses of data in addition to current uses, and second, these policies can vary by state. As a result, fundamental work is being done on how to construct appropriate policies and enforcement mechanisms in this space.

ARL research in trust places it in the context of developing capabilities for continuous monitoring and managing of vulnerabilities and risks in Army's highly heterogeneous networks such as C4ISR[10] networks and broader socio-technical networks. A key risk is the loss of trust in networks. To quantify and model the dynamics of trust in networks, ARL explores socio-cognitive models of trust for achieving fast trust emergence, propagation, and high sustainability. Potential benefits of algorithms based on such theories and models have been demonstrated already in several problems, such as routing of information through networks with nodes of different and uncertain levels of trustworthiness, and detection of cyber-compromise nodes by collaborative assessment of trust by multiple nodes in the network.

NIST's **Security Content Automation Protocol (SCAP) Program** is developing a common framework and language for specifying instructions for security configuration. The program began in response to the Cyber Security R&D Act of 2002 and has since grown to become a suite of specifications that standardize how security configuration information can be communicated to machines and humans. SCAP is capable of describing other security-related attributes and holds the promise of enabling and automating the characterization of Tailored Trustworthy Spaces. Similarly, the ONR **Fabric Project** will provide a software development environment for establishing security guarantees based on explicitly stated security policies.

Spotlight on ONR – Fabric Project

The **Fabric Project** supports the development of strong, principled, security guarantees based on explicitly stated security policies for distributed systems with complex, incomplete, and changing trust between participants. Fabric provides a software development environment to achieve strong security in federated systems, while giving programmers a simple, clear, high-level programming model that frees them from dealing with low-level implementation details. Fabric's platform and application development environment supports securely interconnecting distributed systems, code, and data from different trust domains. In this development environment, all information resources (code and data, both local and remote) look to the programmer like objects, and they are protected in a uniform way using an inherently compositional security mechanism and information flow control. Fabric is freely available, has been used as a teaching tool in many universities, and is being evaluated by government laboratories. The program began in FY 2009 and will continue until FY 2016.

5.1.2.2. Trust Negotiation

The area of Trust Negotiation focuses on frameworks, methods, and technologies to establish trust between system components based on articulated policies via dynamic human-understandable and machine-readable instructions. This requires being able to adjust the assurance level on specific security attributes separately, for example, to establish the differences between an anonymous, low assurance, or high assurance Tailored Trustworthy Space. Future uses of dynamic Tailored Trustworthy Spaces will also require the development of methods to tailor that space given a threat scenario.

Historically, trust negotiation is an area with substantial prior research, which now can be leveraged in the context of Tailored Trustworthy Spaces. Examples of current research in this domain include AFRL's **Trusted Hardware/Secure Processor Program**, which is developing hardware-based roots of trust; ARL's **Trust Management for Optimal Network Performance Program**, whose goal is to enhance distributed decision-making capabilities in the context of network-centric operations by understanding the role trust plays in networks that consist of large systems with complex interactions between communication, information, and social/cognitive networks; and DHS's **Hardware-Enabled Trust Program**.

Spotlight on DHS –
Digital Provenance and Hardware-Enabled Trust Programs

DHS's **Digital Provenance and Hardware-Enabled Trust Programs** develop capabilities to determine the trustworthiness and reliability of data that could have originated from different sources and may have been transformed, processed, aggregated, or otherwise manipulated by many entities. The programs also develop hardware-enabled resilience against all forms of malicious activity. Specifically, the program is researching and developing a digital object tracking platform and tools to fulfill legal and regulatory requirements for evidentiary handling and chain of custody. Under these programs, DHS will develop an end-to-end trust architecture, demonstrate it using a combination of simulated hardware and system prototypes, and test its resilience against attack.

Two awards were made in September 2012 under the DHS 2011 BAA and 2012 SBIR actions. Both projects are developing hardware-based malware defenses. In addition, the BAA work will contribute to hardware defense by developing radically new foundations for end-to-end trust, as well as protection against zero-day hardware exploits. As a result, the protected hardware will exhibit greater resilience and will function effectively, even while under attack.

5.1.2.3. Operations

There are a number of operations that are necessary for dynamic Tailored Trustworthy Spaces, including joining, dynamically tailoring, splitting, merging, and dismantling. These operations are necessary to sustain the "tailoring" of the trustworthy spaces on hand.

Within NSF, the **Secure and Trustworthy Cyberspace (SaTC) Program** funded 21 awards in the Tailored Trustworthy Spaces area in FY 2012, making this theme a significant portion of the SaTC portfolio. In general, there were two categories of such awards: work that establishes the base technology that allows systems to be tailored and specific applications of Tailored Trustworthy Spaces technology to specific environments. An example of the former is a project investigating network-defense systems that adaptively learn "normal" behavior in their deployed environment. One project in the latter group allows for secure and reliable communication across a network whose owner is untrustworthy.

Another example of research in Tailored Trustworthy Spaces operations is the IARPA **Automatic Privacy Protection (APP) Program**, which is developing techniques to provide options for tailoring privacy protection in cyberspace transactions. Additionally, DOE's **Bio-Inspired Technologies for Enhancing Cybersecurity Program** is developing new architectures for implementing cybersecurity policies tailored to different energy system domains.

Spotlight on DOE –
Bio-Inspired Technologies for Enhancing Cybersecurity Program

The DOE **Bio-Inspired Technologies for Enhancing Cybersecurity Program** aims to develop Digital Ants, a biologically inspired cybersecurity solution, and demonstrate that Digital Ants can be successfully deployed across multiple organizational and technological domains found in the energy sector. Digital Ants are designed to leave digital trails in the computer networks whenever they find anomalies or cyber threats, which in turn attract other Ants. Such emergent behavior can dynamically define and adjust cybersecurity policies tailored to individual domains. The Digital Ants project has deployed the framework on multiple platforms and testbeds, from small embedded computers to large computer clusters. The framework has been exercised on up to 20,000 nodes, with plans to scale even larger. Future research will focus on human-assisted automation that will be suitable for utility control room operations.

5.1.2.4. Privacy

Privacy is an important individual and societal concern in the digital age. The ability to achieve and maintain appropriate modes of privacy in cyberspace is challenged by business innovations, rapid technological changes, and sometimes by unintended legal consequences. Cognizant of these challenges, the Federal Government has been a strong advocate of privacy in cyberspace. For example, the Administration's efforts include the President's framework for consumer data privacy.[11] One of the key elements that this framework recognizes is that privacy is dynamic and contextual; privacy determinations always depend on the context in which activities or information disclosures occur. The broader issue of privacy in cyberspace is discussed as a new priority area in Section 6.3.2.

The Tailored Trustworthy Spaces research theme serves as a framework for creating custom cyberspace environments that allow fine-grained control of environmental characteristics for establishing and enforcing desired security and privacy objectives. By tailoring an environment's characteristics and establishing policies for the activities and data encompassed by a Tailored Trustworthy Space (e. g., policies defining access control, identity management, attribution, etc.), the actors also establish the context in which interactions take place. This tailoring capability offers direct support for achieving desirable privacy conditions in cyberspace. One example of research in this area is the IARPA **Security and Privacy Assurance Research (SPAR) Program**, which aims to create practical solutions for secure and private data exchange.

Spotlight on IARPA –
Security and Privacy Assurance Research (SPAR) Program

IARPA started the **Security and Privacy Assurance Research Program** in 2011, building on the success of the past IARPA Automatic

Privacy Protection (APP) Program. The goal of the SPAR Program is to develop and demonstrate practical techniques for data exchange that protect the security and privacy interests of each exchanging party. The program has several phases and will end in FY 2014. The APP Program developed efficient cryptographic protocols for simple queries. The SPAR Program seeks to expand support to complex queries critical to mission applications, while retaining the efficiency demonstrated in the APP Program. SPAR is developing efficient means of protecting security and privacy to allow parties to share just the information that needs to be shared, without risking unnecessary disclosure of sensitive data. The capabilities will allow information access to be tailored to the privileges and need-to-know of parties in a much more granular way than ever before. The data exchange scenarios that will be addressed in the SPAR Program are: complex database queries, publish/subscribe systems, message queue/mailbox systems, and outsourced data storage systems.

5.1.3. Designed-In Security

The vision and goals of the Designed-In Security research theme are as follows:

Vision

Develop the capability to design, implement, and evolve software/hardware systems that are resistant to cyber-attacks, while effectively managing risk, quality, cost, schedule, and complexity. Provide assurance evidence necessary to attest to the level of confidence in the system's ability to withstand attacks.

Goals

- Using assurance-focused engineering practices, languages, and tools, provide the capability to design software systems that are resistant to attacks by dramatically reducing exploitable flaws
- Improve the usability of tools for specifying, implementing, analyzing, and testing attack-resistant software and hardware systems
- Develop the capability to reason about a diversity of assurance attributes (security, safety, reliability, etc.) and the evidence required to achieve the desired confidence in a system's resistance to attacks.

Establishing and maintaining the security (confidentiality, integrity, availability, authentication, non-repudiation) of computer systems has been an objective of the computing field since its inception. Security theory and modeling have evolved in concert with advancements in computing hardware, operating systems, programming languages, and software development methodologies. Foundations for security in computing were put in place in the 1960s and 1970s and were supported by parallel developments in areas such as programming methodologies, program verification, and automated theorem proving. Subsequent interdisciplinary concerns in risk management, privacy, regulatory and standards compliance, and disaster recovery gave rise to information assurance as a field with broader security concerns.

The legacy of security advancements in computing, information assurance, and software assurance has produced many point-solutions, for example, in code analysis or best practices in secure coding. These solutions are valuable, but their effects are limited as the solutions do not scale up to enable capabilities that would allow us to comprehensively design and maintain systems that are resistant to cyber-attacks. Consequently, Federally funded research in Designed-In Security gives priority to achieving progress in the following areas:

- Software development and verification environments
- Assurance evidence and synthesis
- Design tools

5.1.3.1. Software Development and Verification Environments

This area of research creates integrated, security-aware software development environments that can automatically recognize and identify vulnerabilities in code, suggest corrections for identified vulnerabilities, and generate software without code-based vulnerabilities. This area includes research in methods for detecting flaws in software (e.g., formal methods, static or dynamic analysis techniques), improved development tools, such as source code compilers with automatic insertion of constructs that guarantee security and robustness of codes written in unsecured languages, and methods that automatically capture and utilize work flow and design decisions during software coding to aid in the development of functioning systems that meet performance and security requirements.

One focus within these areas is integrating tools into comprehensive development environments that support and assure software design and maintenance across a wide range of security requirements. For example, one of the NSF **SaTC Program** awards in Designed-In Security, titled "High-Level Language Support for Trustworthy Networks," is developing new network programming languages that give programmers the ability to specify what a network should do, separate from how it will be implemented, together with modular constructs that facilitate compositional reasoning about programs. The goal of the project is to transform the way that networks are built by developing network-wide, correct-by-construction programming abstractions and verification tools based on rigorous semantic foundations.

A key feature of security-aware software development and verification environments is usability. The ONR **Software Efficiency Reclamation Program** focuses on enhancing security while also reducing programming complexity through a number of automated processes.

Spotlight on ONR –
Software Efficiency Reclamation Program

The ONR **Software Efficiency Reclamation Program** provides a novel approach for enhancing software execution security and efficiency while preserving programmers' productivity by reducing unnecessary complexity introduced by software development practices. It focuses on reclaiming software execution efficiency by reducing indirection and performing automatic program de-layering and specialization, such that the result is compact and efficient code/executable, with much reduced attack surface and more modest computing resource and energy requirements. This program directly addresses and reduces one of the root causes of software system vulnerability—the complexity of the software. The Software Efficiency Reclamation program was initiated in FY 2013 and will run through FY 2016. It is anticipated that this program will provide a new alternative for deploying software that will allow software customization (for reducing complexity) at installation or pre-execution time, resulting in software that is both more secure and more efficient. The desired contributions of this program are advancements in binary analysis, binary rewriting, program slicing, and program optimization.

5.1.3.2. Assurance Evidence and Synthesis

Assurance evidence and synthesis is a foundational area with the objective of developing systems with provable security properties by achieving a synthesis of system functional specifications, safety and security policies, resource constraints, hardware specifications, and operational environmental descriptions. Key to this effort is the challenge of developing formal methods and models for component architectures that produce desirable safety and security properties in composition with one another. Provable system security properties must be supported by verifiable assurance evidence that is inextricably linked with the system design and can be maintained with the system through its lifecycle. DARPA's **High-Assurance Cyber Military Systems (HACMS) Program** is an example of research in this area, with the objective of achieving automated code synthesis from executable, formal system requirements that include security specifications.

Spotlight on DARPA –
High-Assurance Cyber Military Systems (HACMS) Program

DARPA's **High-Assurance Cyber Military Systems Program** aims to create technology for the construction of high-assurance cyber-physical systems via a clean-slate, formal methods-based approach that enables semi-automated code synthesis from executable, formal specifications. High assurance is defined to mean both functionally correct and satisfying appropriate safety and security properties. Achieving this goal requires a fundamentally different approach from what the software community has taken to date. In addition to a code generator, HACMS seeks a synthesizer capable of producing a machine-checkable proof that assures that the generated code satisfies functional specifications as well as security and safety policies. A key technical challenge is the development of techniques to ensure that the proofs can be composed, allowing the construction of high-assurance systems out of high-assurance components.

5.1.3.3. Design Tools

Tools and the usability of tools for designing secure systems continue to be important areas of research as components of integrated development environments and as instruments for obtaining assurance evidence. The **Secure Coding Initiative (SCI)** at the Software Engineering Institute (SEI) at Carnegie Mellon University, supported by OSD funding, is an example of the development of secure coding standards and supporting tools, such as compilers for the C/C++ programming language. The DOE **Secure Coding for Energy Control Systems Initiative** is leveraging the work done by SEI in secure code development to refine it for use in energy control and delivery systems. Another example is the **Model-Based Evaluation of System Dependability and Security (Mobius) Program**, funded in part by DHS and

DOE, which is developing a toolset that combines attacker, system, and user modeling formalisms, as well as probabilistic evaluation and model composition to allow broad exploration of the system design space for best satisfaction of security requirements.

5.1.4. Cyber Economic Incentives

The vision and goals of the Cyber Economic Incentives research theme are as follows:

Vision

Promote understanding of cyber economic incentives by creating a science-based understanding of markets, decision making, and motivators; promote an environment where deployment of security technology is balanced, providing incentives to engage in responsible behavior and deter criminal and malicious behavior.

Goals

- Develop theories and models of cyber economics and scientific understanding of the social and behavioral dimensions of cybersecurity
- Explore economic models of cybersecurity investments and markets
- Define meaningful cybersecurity metrics and support the collection of cyberspace data (e.g., usage, incidents, attacks, losses) to enable economic, financial, social, and behavioral analyses.

A key objective of the Strategic Plan is to achieve breakthroughs that induce positive changes in cyberspace. The Cyber Economic Incentives research theme aims to induce fundamental changes in cyberspace through economic incentives, broadly encompassing costs and benefits (monetary and otherwise), as well as their allocation, liabilities, and analyses. Without good metrics, processes that enable assured development, sensible and enforceable notions of liability, and mature cost risk analysis methods, the allocation of resources for security will be distorted. Research is needed to develop a sound basis for the economic and social incentives that promote good cybersecurity practices and discourage cybercrime and other bad behavior, and that benefit individuals, organizations, and the larger public good.

As a market, cyberspace suffers from the same inefficiencies observed in other sectors. Some of these inefficiencies include externalities, information asymmetries, and framing effects. Understanding the economic (as well as the social and behavioral) relationships and interactions in cyberspace is a necessary step in facilitating appropriate incentives and enabling effective business decisions to engage in responsible cybersecurity practices.

NSF is at the forefront of Federal research in economic, social, and behavioral influences on cyberspace. Since its FY 2011 **Secure and Trustworthy Cyberspace (SaTC) Program** solicitation, NSF has explicitly supported research in "economic incentives, cybersecurity investments, markets, and motivators." The SaTC Program includes funding for research on the psychological and sociological aspects of cybersecurity decisions and incentives; metrics and data for evaluating and understanding security; behavioral economic analyses of privacy decision making; motivators of insider threat and incentive countermeasures; impacts of trust and institutional design on cybersecurity decisions; incentive structures for cybersecurity in firms and other organizations; and behavioral aspects of real-world vulnerability markets and associated insurance/software-derivative instruments. This program is laying the foundation for research in cyber economics by explicitly funding multidisciplinary investigations that bring together computer science, economics, and behavioral sciences researchers. In FY 2012, SaTC funded 18 Cyber-Economic Incentive awards, making this theme a significant portion of the SaTC portfolio. Topics of these awards included understanding the malware economy, understanding how to deter malicious activities, and pricing strategies for Smart Grid systems that cause the systems to stabilize.

DHS, through its 2011 BAA, has initiated a **Cyber Economics Incentives Program** to develop new theories and models of cyber economics and a scientific understanding of the social dimensions of cyber economics. This program will reexamine scientific frameworks to incentivize vendors of cyberspace-related technologies (e.g., encourage use of secure software engineering and analysis practices, and software vulnerability detection) and security incident forensics through acquisition, regulation, and standards.

In addition to the broader cyber economic programs implemented by NSF and DHS, agencies have implemented targeted research programs focusing on studying the details of the economic models behind security challenges of particular concern; for example, ONR is conducting in-depth research on the underground economies supporting botnets.

Spotlight on ONR –
Infiltration of Botnet Command-and-Control and Support Ecosystems Project through the Multidisciplinary University Research Initiative (MURI)

The ONR **Infiltration of Botnet Command-and-Control and Support Ecosystems** project through the **Multidisciplinary University Research Initiative (MURI)** was started in FY 2009 with the objective of increasing our understanding of cyberspace underground economics and to provide insights on how to curb some of the activities. In addition to exploring the economics behind the cyberspace underground, the program is investigating techniques for infiltration of botnet command and control structures, for automated analysis of malware binaries, and applications of natural-language processing to gain insights from human communications that support the botnet ecosystem. The program is scheduled for completion in FY 2014.

5.2. Developing Scientific Foundations

The research themes within the Inducing Change thrust focus on near-term threats and current or near-horizon challenges and technologies. In addition to these efforts, the Federal Government must also provide investments for laying the theoretical, empirical, computational, and data mining foundations needed to meet needs arising from next-generation technologies and to address the threats of the future. Developing a strong, rigorous scientific foundation to cybersecurity helps the field in the following ways:

- **Organizes disparate areas of knowledge**: Provides structure and organization to a broad-based body of knowledge in the form of testable models and predictions
- **Enables discovery of universal laws**: Produces laws that express an understanding of basic, universal dynamics against which to test problems and formulate explanations
- **Applies the rigor of the scientific method**: Approaches problems using a systematic methodology and discipline to formulate hypotheses, design and execute repeatable experiments, and collect and analyze data

5.2.1. Foundations for Science of Security

Agencies have already begun support for research aimed at developing a cyber-science base, or "a science of security." Programs within a growing group of agencies are now providing funding for research on difficult scientific problems, such as system composition and measurement, as well as supporting the formation of a community of practice centered upon the creation of a scientific base.

The Air Force Office of Scientific Research (AFOSR), ARL, NSA, and NSF have a coordinated Science of Security effort underway. In FY 2010, AFOSR, NSA, and NSF developed a set of research objectives to advance the science of security and then supported these objectives by funding several related research projects. Later, in FY 2011, AFOSR awarded a five-year-long MURI on the "**Science of Cyber Security Modeling, Composition, and Measurement**." The purpose of this MURI is to advance the scientific basis for trustworthiness by developing concepts, relationships, and laws with predictive value that focus on security modeling, composition, and measurement. Complementary to these activities, ARL has a **Science for Cyber** portfolio focused on developing novel theoretical constructs that can enable future cybersecurity advances. Programs in the portfolio explore models for the representation of cybersecurity, ensemble techniques for improved detection of attacks, and behavior as a fundamental indicator in detection and analysis. In particular, the research program focuses on theories and models that will lead to more effective intrusion detection techniques.

In February 2014, NSA awarded four universities with funding to create four "science of security" research centers, which are termed "lablets." The lablets will jump-start multidisciplinary, multifaceted collaborative research in five key areas of security: scalability and composability, policy governed secure collaboration, predictive security metrics, resilient architectures, and human behavior and usability. Because there are many possible and different paths towards creating a security science, early stages of this work will be directed at exploring a wide variety of methods and building a large community to support this field.

Public comments have stressed that the Strategic Plan should include greater exploration of the role that the field of cryptographic design can play in addressing the central challenges of cybersecurity. Advances in cryptography (e.g., fully homomorphic encryption) will continue to play an important role in the building of fundamentally secure cyber solutions. Research activities in both the Designed-In Security theme and Developing Scientific Foundations thrust reflect the need for and importance of research on rigorous and formal foundations for achieving security. In FY 2012, 35 of NSF's SaTC awards focused on advancing the foundations of the field, with theoretical cryptography representing a large portion of the awards made. Other topics of research included programming language semantics that specifically seek to capture security-related behavior, cloud computing on encrypted data, and methods for incorporating real world data into scientific security research in a way that respects privacy concerns. For example, NSF SaTC awards for a project called Critter@Home, inspired by SETI@Home, allow individual computer users to gather security information that can be queried in a distributed but privacy-preserving manner, allowing researchers to find out what is happening at end-user computers in near real time. Since the raw data never leaves the individual's computer, many privacy issues are avoided.

Spotlight on NSF –
Secure and Trustworthy Cyberspace (SaTC) Program

In strong alignment with the themes outlined in the Strategic Plan, the NSF SaTC program's approach to research, development, and education leverages the disciplines of mathematics and statistics, the social, behavioral, and economic sciences, and engineering together with the computing, communications, and information sciences. Spanning NSF's Directorates for Computer and Information Science and Engineering (CISE), Education and Human Resources (EHR), Engineering (ENG), Mathematical and Physical Sciences (MPS), and Social, Behavioral & Economic Sciences (SBE), the multidisciplinary SaTC portfolio currently comprises approximately 650 active awards that range from seedling grants (typically around $150K/18 months) to large-scale, multi-institution *Frontier* awards (up to $10M/5 years). The **Frontier awards** SaTC awarded in FY 2013 were:

The **Rethinking Security in the Era of Cloud Computing** project, dubbed Project Silver and led by University of North Carolina at Chapel Hill, seeks to exploit the opportunities inherent in leveraging cloud providers as trusted partners to improve tenant security. The project convenes periodic "Cloud Security Horizons" summits with industry stakeholders to help shape the future of security in the cloud.

The **Trustworthy Health and Wellness** (THaW) project led by Dartmouth College includes experts from computer science, business, behavioral health, health policy, and healthcare information technology. The project is tackling the challenges of providing trustworthy information systems for health and wellness given that sensitive information and health-related tasks are being increasingly pushed to mobile devices and cloud-based services.

The **Usable Privacy Policy Project** led by Carnegie Mellon University is developing scalable technologies for extracting key privacy policy features semi-automatically from website privacy policies, thereby helping users understand the privacy provided by websites before disclosing their information. This project includes transitioning their technology into open source browsers.

During FY 2013 and FY 2014, SaTC initiated a series of seedling grants seeking to catalyze new collaborations between computer scientists and social scientists, with the goal of increasing the pool of interdisciplinary research. Among the topics being explored by the inaugural set of grants in FY 2013 are frameworks for Moving Target defense, using new visualization methods to improve passwords, user-tailored privacy and security systems, and assessing cybercrime vulnerability.

FY 2013 also marked the addition of the EHR Directorate to the SaTC solicitation, and 12 new cybersecurity education research projects were funded. Among these are a healthcare-based cybersecurity competition designed to bring young women into the field; a "build it, break it, fix it" competition to encourage not just breaking into, but also improving systems; a cybersecurity education center targeted toward veterans; and an effort focused on curriculum development for cyber-physical systems security and privacy education.

In addition to the initiatives described previously, which are broader-scoped explorations of the scientific foundations of security, agencies, such as AFRL, have also created programs and solicitations that explore foundational research in security with the end goal of supporting their explicit mission needs.

Spotlight on AFRL –
Cyber Assurance Technologies Solicitation

Many of the research projects for the AFRL "Invent Foundations of Trust and Assurance" strategic objective are funded through the AFRL **Cyber Assurance Technologies Solicitation** issued in FY 2011. "Invent Foundations of Trust and Assurance" is one of AFRL's four primary strategic goals for cybersecurity research. The end goal of this strategy is to provide the Air Force with capabilities to mitigate supply chain intervention and to establish hardware and software roots-of-trust; to create the foundations of trust for applications, functions, and missions; and to develop the mathematical algebra to represent missions, applications, and infrastructure for provably correct mission characterizations in contested environments. AFRL will use a scientific characterization of cyberinfrastructure relative to mission functionality and criticality to focus and prioritize the efforts toward developing assured, verifiable, and trusted hardware and software.

5.2.2. Metrics, Models, and Experiments

Cybersecurity metrics make up another major area of interest in agency programs supporting the science of security. Multiple public comments highlighted cybersecurity metrics as a key area for foundational research and development. Currently, two major research activities are underway that focus on cybersecurity metrics: the OSD **Cyber Measurement Campaign (CMC)** and the DOE **CyberPhysical Survivability Metrics Program**. The DOE program seeks to develop a suite of metrics and models for assessing, comparing, and gaining actionable insight into the cyber-physical survivability properties of large-scale, highly networked energy delivery systems. The metrics and models will provide the capabilities to evaluate, quantify, and improve the survivability of existing delivery systems and to engineer new systems that exhibit the intended survivability properties in the context of explicit engineering tradeoffs.

Spotlight on OSD –
Cyber Measurement Campaign (CMC)

OSD's **Cyber Measurement Campaign** was launched in August 2011 and is scheduled to continue until FY 2015. The end goal of the campaign is to develop a suite of metrics to define hypothesis-driven experiments that measure key cybersecurity capabilities. There are three aspects to the CMC: Cyber Technology Measurement, Cyber Range Fidelity Measurement, and Experimental Infrastructure. Initial experiments focus on quantifying cyber-resiliency with mature research prototypes, as well as measuring resulting improvements to cybersecurity. For example, one of the initial experiments already conducted tested the hypothesis that increasing an attacker's uncertainty increases workload. The test used ARCSYNE technology to create an IP hopping defense in a closed community of interest. The results showed a dramatic increase in the time and workload required to execute a successful attack. So far, simple scenarios have been used to generate initial results. Growth into complex operational scenarios with realistic settings will enable the derivation of general models and metrics.

5.3. Maximizing Research Impact

Maximizing the impact of research outlined in the game-changing R&D themes will require cooperation between government and private sector communities, collaboration across international borders, integration of output across research themes, and the support of national priorities such as health IT and Smart Grid systems. As President Obama said in May 2009, "America's economic prosperity in the 21st century will depend on cybersecurity."

5.3.1. Integrating Research Efforts and Engaging the Research Community

DoD OSD's **Cyber Applied Research and Advanced Development Program** supports integration across multiple cybersecurity research themes. This program funds DoD laboratories and the NSA to develop technological solutions that can be applied across cyber operations. This research effort enhances and extends the work of individual laboratories and encourages cross-laboratory collaboration.

To facilitate exchange and collaboration by the broader scientific cyber research community and to support peer-reviewed research communities in areas not served by mainstream organizations, the Office of the Director of National Intelligence (ODNI) has created a new **Journal of Sensitive Cybersecurity Research and Engineering (JSCoRE)**. The new journal allows the secure dissemination of peer-reviewed, high-quality, and sensitive cybersecurity research to governmental, commercial, and academic communities with appropriate security clearance accesses.

A number of workshops are organized by agencies to engage the research community. Some examples include the DHS Cybersecurity Applications and Technology Conference for Homeland Security, DHS/DoD Small Business Innovation Research (SBIR) Conference, DHS/NIST/NSA Annual IT Security Automation Conference, DHS/NIST/NSA/NSF/OSD National Initiative for Cybersecurity Education Annual Workshop, DHS/GSA/NIST Cloud Forums, NIST/NSA Mobile Security Forum, NSF Workshops on Incorporating Security Concepts in Undergraduate Computer Science Curriculum, NSF

Workshop on Multi-spectrum Metrics for Cyber Defense, NSF/National Laboratories Workshop on the Human Dimensions in Cyber Operations R&D Priorities, DHS/NSF Cybersecurity Insurance Workshop, DHS IT Security Entrepreneur Forum, Innovation Summit, SINET Showcase, and Transition To Practice Showcase, NSA Science of Security Workshop, DHS/DOE Trustworthy Cyber Infrastructure for the Power Grid (TCIPG) Industry Workshops, and ODNI Workshops on Computational Cybersecurity in Compromised Environments.

Supporting the development of technical standards is another area of how agencies collaborate with industry. For example, NIST and NSA have been developing, maintaining, and coordinating validation programs for cryptographic standards; NIST, NSA, and OSD participate in Internet Engineering Task Force (IETF) security groups to develop standard representations and corresponding reference implementations of security-relevant data; and NIST and DOE/OE support the development of Smart Grid standards through the Smart Grid Interoperability Panel (SGIP) Cyber Security Working Group (CSWG).

In addition to domestic programs, Federal research agencies support and fund collaborative cybersecurity R&D with a number of international partners. Public comments have noted that there are a host of cybersecurity R&D-related issues that must be discussed in an international context, including how international efforts in innovative technologies impact the development of the U.S. cybersecurity efforts; and how international technical requirements affect American companies, create trade barriers, and impact public procurement practices. We note that the U.S. *International Strategy for Cyberspace*[12] defines the strategic and policy objectives for the U.S. Government in engaging international partners on a range of cyber issues. This strategy will also guide cybersecurity R&D efforts that engage international partners or stakeholders.

The DoD has a number of international partnerships such as **The Technical Cooperation Program (TTCP)**. TTCP is a 50-year-old military R&D Memorandum of Understanding among the countries of Australia, Canada, New Zealand, the United Kingdom, and the United States designed to support cooperation on research to reduce duplication of effort and maximize mutual benefits. The Command, Control, Communications, and Information Systems (C3I) Group within TTCP addresses technologies to achieve interoperable, seamless information systems focused on the support of allied military missions. Technical Panel 11 focuses on the areas of information assurance and defensive information warfare.

Other DoD international partnerships include the Network and Information Sciences **International Technology Alliance (ITA)**, a collaborative research alliance between the UK Ministry of Defense (UK MoD) and ARL, and a consortium of leading academic and industry partners. Now in its seventh year, ITA continues to support research on secure data sharing and collaboration among coalition partners. In 2010, ONR's Global Division opened a new international science and technology office in Prague, Czech Republic. The Prague office established a regional presence for the U.S. Navy within the eastern Europe international science and technology community. The Czech-ONR Global relationship includes joint research in a number of cyber technologies, such as Multi Agent Systems (with a focus on adversarial reasoning, distributed control systems, and distributed computing).

Further strengthening international engagements, DHS has initiated jointly funded projects with U.S. partners. Currently, Australia, UK, Canada, the Netherlands, Sweden, Germany, and Israel co-fund projects within the DHS S&T 2011 Cyber BAA. Additionally, NSF supports collaborative research in computer science and cybersecurity between researchers in the U.S. and Israel through the United States-Israel Binational Science Foundation (BSF).

In November 2006 and April 2007, two International Cooperation in Trustworthy, Secure and Dependable ICT Infrastructures (INCO-TRUST) workshops were held with researchers from the EU, US, Australia, Japan, and Canada who engaged within ICT Trust, Security and Dependability. These workshops were highly successful in their mission of identifying and scoping research areas that require and will benefit from international collaboration between EU researchers and those within other industrialized nations.[13] More recently, out of the connections that were established through INCOTRUST, NSF Principal Investigators have participated in the European Union's Building International Cooperation for Trustworthy ICT (BIC) project.

5.3.2. Supporting National Priorities

The 2011 Strategic Plan outlined several activities already underway at agencies that targeted national priorities with substantial cybersecurity influences. Since the release of the Plan, several agencies have expanded on these cybersecurity tracks and started new programs that focus on applied cybersecurity research in national priority fields.[14]

Privacy and security concerns must be satisfied in the use of valuable health information. The **Strategic Healthcare IT Advanced Research Projects on Security (SHARPS) Program** of the Office of the National Coordinator for Health Information Technology (ONC) focuses on advancing the requirements, foundations, design, development and deployment of security, privacy tools, and methods for electronic health records, health information exchanges, and telemedicine. For example, the SHARPS Program is applying state-of-the-art techniques in encryption, ciphertext policy, and decryption based on biomarkers to safeguard data transmitted by electronic health record systems and health information exchanges. Complementary to SHARPS is NIST's **Health IT Security Program**, which focuses on solutions that enable interoperability and adoption of health IT technologies. For example, using security automation specifications (a research area within Tailored Trustworthy Spaces), the Health IT Security Program accelerates the deployment of health IT platforms by enabling automated security certification to Health Insurance Portability and Accountability Act (HIPAA) regulations.

NIST also initiated and chaired the Smart Grid Interoperability Panel Cybersecurity Committee (SGCC), which led the collaboration between the private sector, academia, national research laboratories, and Federal agencies in facilitating the development of cybersecurity standards for the Smart Grid. For example, similar to NIST's work in Health IT and cybersecurity, SGCC developed the NISTIR 7628, "Guidelines for Smart Grid Cybersecurity," which is being used globally as a foundational tool for helping to secure the Smart Grid. In January 2013, the Smart Grid Interoperability Panel (SGIP) fully transitioned to a private/public partnership funded by industry stakeholders in cooperation with the Federal Government. NIST continues to have an active role in SGIP. Current news and member information now reside at http://www.sgip.org/.

Similarly, DOE research efforts advancing the goals of the 2011 Roadmap to Achieve Energy Delivery Systems Cybersecurity[15] utilize multiple Tailored Trustworthy Spaces concepts. These efforts include SIEGate, an information exchange gateway that provides secure data communication between control centers; Secure and Real-time Communication Substrate, a trustworthy cyber infrastructure and technologies for wide-area monitoring, control, and active energy demand management; and Trust Anchors, which are monitoring and control devices that independently verify systems function, reveal deceptive malicious function, attest to system state, and verify correctness of system tests. The alignment of Tailored Trustworthy Spaces and cybersecurity R&D in the energy sector was explored at the NITRD Workshop on Tailored Trustworthy Spaces: Solutions for the Smart Grid on July 2011 in Washington, DC.

NSF's SaTC Program supports security research related to many of the cyber-physical systems that make up the critical infrastructure supporting multiple national priority areas, such as biomedical devices, the Smart Grid, transportation systems, and environment monitoring. SaTC also supports the Administration's focus on education by funding the NSF **CyberCorps: Scholarship for Service Program**, which sustains efforts to establish curricula for new courses, degree programs, and pathways in cybersecurity education. Public comments on the Strategic Plan have emphasized the importance of training: the Plan and associated research must include training and the training should integrate the results of research to help the workforce adopt new technologies and practices.

Spotlight on NSF –
CyberCorps®:
Scholarships for Service

The goal of the **CyberCorps®: Scholarship for Service (SFS) Program**, administered by NSF and supported by the Office of Personnel Management and DHS, is to educate, recruit, and retain the next generation of cybersecurity professionals. NSF issues grants to colleges and universities for student scholarships in support of education in areas relevant to cybersecurity. In return for their scholarships, recipients agree to work after graduation for the Federal Government, a State, Local, or Tribal government in a position related to cybersecurity for a period equal to the length of the scholarship.

As of April 2014, there were 51 SFS scholarship institutions with more than 460 active scholarships awarded to undergraduate and graduate students. The first SFS graduates entered the Federal workforce in 2002 and since then over 2,000 students (24% bachelors, 73% masters, and 3% doctoral degrees) have been admitted to the SFS program with 1536 completing their degrees. SFS scholarship recipients have been placed in internships and full-time positions in more than 120 Federal agencies and departments, including the NSA, the CIA, and the Departments of Defense, Treasury, Commerce, Homeland Security, and Justice as well as in State, Local, or Tribal governments. The overall placement rate of the SFS program is 93 percent.

The top enrolling SFS institution has been the University of Tulsa where each student is assigned to a Tulsa police crime lab on campus to perform forensics on digital devices. In 2003, SFS students contributed to a triple homicide investigation by tracing email communication from victims to the perpetrator. Another unique feature of the Tulsa program is the presence of the U.S. Secret Service facility on campus where SFS students have collaborated with U.S. Secret Service agents to develop new ways for recovering data from more than 5,000 damaged cellphones, GPS, and other devices.

5.4. Accelerating Transition to Practice

An explicit, coordinated process that transitions the fruits of research into practice is essential if Federal cybersecurity R&D investments are to have significant, long-lasting impacts. Currently, a chasm exists between the research community, which focuses on exercising research components in demonstration environments, and the operations community, which acquires system prototypes containing research components and implements them in operational environments. Bridging that chasm, colloquially referred to as the "valley of death," requires cooperative efforts and investments by both the R&D and operations communities, and may involve risk-taking on the part of the private sector as it shepherds research results through the commercialization process. The Strategic Plan called out the need to have activities around discovering technology; testing and evaluation; and transition, adoption, and commercialization.

5.4.1. A Platform for Transitioning Research to Practice

In February 2012, DHS S&T initiated the **Transition to Practice (TTP) Program** with the mission of identifying promising federally funded cybersecurity research that can be transitioned to the private sector for commercialization in 24-36 months. DHS is partnering with agencies across the Federal R&D community, focusing on the DOE national labs in FY 2012 to identify eight mature technologies that address existing or imminent cybersecurity gaps in public or private systems impacting national security. The TTP Program funds test and evaluation, red-teaming, pilots, and incremental improvements to research technologies, thereby filling an incubator role that has been lacking in the transition of Federal R&D. Additionally, the program may assist in funding the commercialization efforts of technologies that have successful test and evaluation, red-teaming, and pilot deployments. In FY 2013, TTP hosted the first annual Federal Government Technology Demonstration Day to showcase the eight technologies identified in FY 2012, and began the process toward building pilots based on these technologies. TTP also hosted a Technology Demonstration Day for the finance sector to attract pilot partners in this area of critical infrastructure, along with Investor, Integrator and IT Company Forums in Washington, D.C. and Silicon Valley to showcase the technologies and attract commercialization partners. Public comments have stressed that successful and efficient transition to practice requires dialogue between the 'suppliers' and 'customers' of the research, i.e., between university and laboratory researchers and industry technologists.

The OSD ASD(R&E) Cyber Transition to Practice (CTP) initiative focuses on moving cyber S&T into DoD operations, i.e., overcoming the well-known "valley of death" for S&T. Transitioning cyber S&T is challenging because it is typically software intensive, exhibits cross-cutting dependencies, inhabits a rapidly evolving landscape, and is immature when it emerges from laboratory R&D efforts. The CTP initiative matures and transitions cyber S&T through range-based test and evaluation, operational pilots, and SBIR phase 2E projects. The CTP initiative is focusing initially on DoD Laboratories, Federally Funded Research and Development Centers (FFRDC), and University Affiliated Research Centers (UARC) as sources of cyber S&T to transition to combatant commands, the DoD Services, and other government agencies.

Addressing the "valley of death" between academic research results and commercialization, the NSF SaTC Program includes a Transition to Practice perspective that provides funding for later phases of a research and development lifecycle, including applied research, prototyping, experimental deployment, and early adoption activities. In addition to the broader transition to practice programs listed above, there are a variety of activities that focus on transfer models for technologies that improve the security of currently deployed infrastructure and products, some of which are listed in the following section. Another mechanism for engagement of industry is the NSF Industry/University Cooperative Research Center (I/UCRC) Program: NSF supports a center called the Security & Software Engineering Research Center (S2ERC) that focuses on promoting industry and academic collaboration in the areas of security and software engineering. This center currently includes Ball State University, Iowa State University, and Virginia Polytechnic Institute, and is growing.

As a counterpoint, public comments have noted that academia is motivated today by disruptive technology transfer models where game-changing ideas can be commercialized with relatively small amounts of investment through start-up companies, and that technology transfer models are needed where solutions can be integrated into existing industry products and services for sustaining impact.

5.4.2. Unique Paths for Differing Technologies

Several agencies have also started broader transition to practice programs that encompass all aspects of the Accelerating Transition to Practice thrust, but have focused on certain types of technologies or on technologies with similar, but unique characteristics for implementation. For example, the AFRL **Next-Generation Cyber Warriors Initiative** selects, educates, trains, and augments cyber warriors for superior performance. The goal of this initiative is to develop and transition the technologies and identify the human skill sets needed to address key technical challenge areas related to optimizing our future cyber warriors: visualization, skill-augmentation, cyber education, and training.

NIST established the **National Cybersecurity Center of Excellence (NCCoE)** through a partnership with the State of Maryland and Montgomery County. The NCCoE is dedicated to furthering innovation through the rapid identification, integration, and adoption of practical, standards-based cybersecurity solutions. The center provides an environment that encourages interaction among businesses and solution providers, increases opportunities for innovation, and advances the current understanding of cybersecurity technology capabilities and costs. Initial focus areas include healthcare information exchanges and securing assets for the financial services sector. The NCCoE is also advancing building blocks of cybersecurity solutions that are applicable across multiple industry sectors.

DARPA and NSA have created programs that act as platforms for producing cybersecurity technologies with rapid turnaround times. In FY 2013, DARPA operated the **Cyber Fast Track (CFT) Program**, to build cybersecurity capabilities on an agile, quick-response basis, and to fund smaller cyber projects that result in rapid development of cyber technologies with potential for large payoffs. NSA's **Applied Research Prototypes Program** is designed to facilitate new industry engagements by funding short-turnaround cybersecurity technology R&D, with demonstrable prototypes delivered within three months of project initiation.

6. ASSESSING THE FEDERAL RESPONSE TO THE STRATEGIC PLAN

This section provides an analysis of the Federal response to the 2011 Strategic Plan and suggestions for additional areas of emphasis and research that are needed to adapt to broader changes in the cybersecurity landscape. Section 6.1 examines the sufficiency of the Federal response to the Strategic Plan, analyzing where overlap and gaps exist in current R&D activities. The analysis is based on NITRD coordination activities, agency feedback, and public comments. Section 6.2 lists technology areas that are currently within the scope of the Strategic Plan, but could benefit from additional emphasis. Section 6.3 describes two new major research areas for the Strategic Plan.

The analysis in Sections 6.2 and 6.3 considers public comments and whether ongoing research adequately supports Administration positions and initiatives established since publication of the Strategic Plan, including:

- The Administration's five priority areas of action for cybersecurity:
- Protect Critical Infrastructure
- Improve Incident Reporting and Response
- Secure Federal Networks
- Engage Internationally
- Shape the Future
- Executive Order 13636 (EO 13636) "Improving Critical Infrastructure Cybersecurity"
- Presidential Policy Directive 21 (PPD-21) "Critical Infrastructure Security and Resilience"
- The Administration's goals for cybersecurity legislation

6.1. Sufficiency of the Federal Response

Overall, each thrust and theme has multiagency participation and support. While many programs address similar scientific thematic areas, the key areas of those programs are shaped by the unique mission needs of the different agencies. For example, even though NSF, NIST, and AFRL have each implemented Transition to Practice programs, NSF's program focuses on transitioning academic research results to commercialization; NIST's program fosters deployment and adoption of tools to enhance consumer confidence in

IT systems; and AFRL trains cyber warriors in newly developed cybersecurity technologies.

The R&D outlined in the 2011 Strategic Plan is well-matched by agency efforts, with relatively few gaps and little overlap, given the overall level of Federal funding of cybersecurity R&D. One area of R&D that could benefit from additional emphasis is the Cyber Economic Incentives theme. Both DHS and NSF offer broadly scoped research programs in this area, which have contributed to progress in fundamental research. However, as with ONR's research on botnets, other agencies may benefit from activities that rigorously examine the economic basis of specific cyber threats that align with their missions.

6.2. Technology Areas for Additional Emphasis

The Strategic Plan's R&D framework encompasses a broad set of research topics and technologies. Since its introduction at the end of 2011, the Plan has elicited comments from the public, inputs from other Federal reports and strategy documents, and responses from agency experts. These inputs have guided the identification of research topics that could benefit from additional, specific emphasis.

6.2.1. Within Moving Target

6.2.1.1. Situational Awareness and Cyber Instrumentation

Situational awareness is critical in order to understand the current state in a network or system and to determine appropriate courses of action. Without situational awareness, real-time critical asset management cannot take place effectively. Situational awareness is made possible by cyber instrumentation, which provides the core underlying technology by which the diverse mechanisms and strategies that increase system resiliency and agility are measured. If the network or a system is not adequately instrumented, it is difficult to determine the effectiveness of a technology in either avoiding or resisting an attack and in adjusting active responses in near real-time.

6.2.2. Within Tailored Trustworthy Spaces

6.2.2.1. Roots of Trust

Modern computing devices consist of various hardware and software components at multiple layers of abstraction. Existing security measurement and protection systems are rooted in software, but the results of these measurements are not always dependable because they rely on the integrity of all underlying hardware components, many of which do not have a firm basis of trustworthiness. While trust in the multiple layers of a computing device can be built up through an iterative process of verifying successive levels, there must be an initial source of trust—the "root of trust"—in a system that is implicitly trustworthy.

Emerging classes of hardware components may provide the basis for dependable security measurements. These trusted hardware components generally include tamper-proof storage, which can be used to protect sensitive cryptographic keys, measurements of integral software components, and limited cryptographic functionality to perform device authentication operations. Research is needed to evaluate the utility and limitations of trusted hardware components with respect to performance of basic security measurements. In addition to establishing a solid foundation for fundamental security metrics, the research should include mechanisms for validating security measurements from the hardware to the software layer. This research would also contribute to the "composition problem," where security metrics are computed for a system composed of verifiably trusted components. See the "Composition and Compromised Systems" section below.

6.2.2.2. Trusted Identities for People, Machines, and Programs

The **National Strategy for Trusted Identities in Cyberspace (NSTIC) Program** is managing a portfolio of pilot projects that advance the theory and practice of trusted identities. Adoption of the Personal Identity Verification (PIV) card for logical access (i.e., access to IT resources) has been identified as a key metric in the *Cross Agency Goal: Cybersecurity* for 2013. Research initiatives that address impediments to deployment of PIV-based applications are critical to enhancing the security of Federal IT infrastructure. Such initiatives would also advance the NSTIC vision by demonstrating the utility of multi-factor authentication.

NSTIC's focus is on trusted identities for human users, but emerging computing environments are presenting new authentication requirements. As the "Internet of Things" begins to take shape, a need for trusted machine identities has become apparent. While there are innovative technologies on the horizon, additional research is required to determine which system properties should be assessed for monitoring.

6.2.2.3. New Technologies for Cyber Supply Chain Risk Management

Design and manufacture of computing and communications hardware and software are done globally, and the supply chains for the cyberinfrastructure that runs our Nation are now built from diverse interactions among suppliers, integrators, and servicers. Maintaining the security of the Nation's cyber infrastructure requires developing ways of validating and assuring the security of complex hardware and software systems featuring subcomponents that can come from a wide set of sources, each within different kinds of systems with differing requirements for risk tolerances. Public comments note that novel strategies are needed for improving security of integrated circuit and microprocessor design and manufacture, and that specification and verification should be expanded to include security properties. Solving cyber supply chain risk management problems requires an active policy and regulatory response working in tandem with research and development to mitigate these risks. An example of a nascent R&D effort in this area is the DARPA **Supply Chain Hardware Integrity for Electronics Defense (SHIELD) Program**, which seeks develop an advanced supply chain hardware authentication technology capability.

6.2.2.4. New Technologies for Information Sharing

Our national critical infrastructures are composed from a variety of smaller systems, the majority of which are privately owned. Information sharing among private sector operators, and among private sector owners and the government, has emerged as a key component of our long range security plans. However, effective information sharing in current legal frameworks demands controls on data that do not exist today, or are expensive to implement. Technologies to control the secondary flow of information or to anonymize data in a cost-effective manner are urgently needed to implement policy goals.

6.2.3. Within Designed-in Security

6.2.3.1. Composition and Compromised Systems

The creation of provably correct systems is a long held objective, but current methods do not scale to practical applications. Modern IT systems are highly complex, with millions of lines of code in the operating system alone. Current methods will not support the production of high-reliability systems with this level of complexity.

New software engineering methods are needed to support the production of high-reliability system specifications and of their provably correct transformation into deployable systems. There is also a need for techniques that support formal composition of high-scale and high-complexity systems to avoid emergent behaviors.

In the past, research into composition focused exclusively on systems composed of trustworthy, or at least unaltered, components. Unfortunately, alteration of one or more components in a system is all too common. An important new area of research is the composition of systems in which one or more components is assumed to be compromised. Developing systems that continue to operate correctly after being compromised is one promising opportunity to shift the cost ratio in the favor of the defender.

6.2.3.2. Architectural Resiliency

Research into fundamentally new approaches for the design of architectures underlying cyberinfrastructure is necessary so that these architectures can be made truly resilient to cyber-attack, natural disaster, and inadvertent failure. In particular, research is needed to identify and evaluate network architectures that feature a survivable core, and to develop algorithms to bootstrap widespread network restoration from this core.

6.2.4. Within Developing Scientific Foundations

6.2.4.1. Cyber Experimentation and Simulation

The role of cyber experimentation, testing, analysis, and evaluation leading to deployment of technologies is a critical element in delivering working solutions. Public comments note the importance of computational sciences and applied mathematics in understanding complex systems; comments push for the development of new tools that can be used for predictive modeling and simulation of complex systems, mathematical analysis of the behavior of complex systems, and use of models of complex systems to inform policy makers.

Our ability to conduct and learn from cyber experiments is currently underdeveloped. Similarly, in light of the growing demands to secure and defend increasingly complex cyber systems, our capabilities in cyber and cyber-physical modeling and in simulation of large-scale operations or cyber-physical systems need improvements. For instance, we need higher-fidelity capabilities to model threats and attacks in order to determine their impacts on the execution of national security missions or on the operations of critical infrastructures in the private sector.

6.2.4.2. Security Metrics

Security metrics present a target-rich opportunity for researchers. As the community shifts from a checklist-based approach to a "security culture," additional work in security metrics is required to transition from tactical metrics (e.g., compliance) to more holistic measurements, such as measuring the health of a network. Public comments emphasize the need for "metrics/benchmarks of security and trustworthiness" for hardware security as well as software security. Other opportunities for metrics target specific government and industry requirements. For example, the Administration identified improving incident reporting and response as one of the five priority areas for action. However, the associated metrics are insufficient to measure the degree of improvement. Similar opportunities exist for metrics associated with measuring the return on investment for both operational decisions and research investments.

6.3. Additional Prospective Research Areas

The framework for Federal cybersecurity R&D articulated in the 2011 Strategic Plan is not static; the framework and priorities are expected to evolve as our understanding of challenges and solutions improves. In looking forward, several broad areas of research have emerged as candidates for coordinated, multiagency efforts. While discussion of prospective research areas continues and a decision on priorities remains, examples of additional research that may strengthen the goals of the Strategic Plan are provided below.

6.3.1. Security of Cyber-Physical Systems

Our increasing reliance on cyber-physical systems, in which computing, cyberspace, and control of physical processes are interconnected, requires commensurate advances to secure them and to improve their trustworthiness. Such systems are part of the fabric of modern economies and provide critical functions in areas such as the generation and delivery of electricity, management of transportation systems, and the delivery of medical and emergency care.

Cyber-physical systems operate under constraints arising from the requirements of the physical processes being controlled. Cyber-physical systems are a significant challenge because the traditional ordering of cybersecurity priorities does not hold. Historically, computer systems are designed to meet confidentiality and integrity requirements, with availability as the distant third. For cyber-physical systems, which may be controlling the shut-off valve in a power plant or a water system, availability is often the most important requirement. There are also real-time requirements and other subtleties that differentiate these systems from the cyber world. In the energy sector, for example, stringent, millisecond operational requirements of energy delivery systems cannot be affected adversely by security technologies. Cybersecurity solutions that are developed to protect business systems and networks may not be appropriate for cyber-physical systems; additional research is needed to address requirements specific to these systems.

6.3.2. Privacy and Protected Disclosure

The January 2013 President's Council of Advisors on Science and Technology (PCAST) report on the NITRD Program[16] cited privacy and protected disclosure as a cross-cutting theme, "one that is important for every agency and mission, as huge amounts of diverse information about individuals become available in online electronic form." Multiple public comments emphasized the need for privacy research to address both how the public perceives privacy in the context of cybersecurity and how new cybersecurity technologies and practices can integrate privacy.

As highlighted in the PCAST report, a major challenge is that "no agency has primary responsibility for privacy R&D, although many agencies need a better understanding of the science of privacy and protected disclosure in an online digital world." Development of the scientific and engineering foundations of privacy R&D will require multiagency collaboration.

While some aspects of privacy are included in the scope of the Tailored Trustworthy Spaces theme, there are additional challenges that can be addressed through targeted R&D investment. The challenges, as outlined in the PCAST report, include realizing the benefits of collective personal information without compromising the privacy of individuals, achieving cybersecurity and security more broadly without unnecessary disclosure of individual information, designing systems to avoid unintended personal disclosure, empowering individuals to assert their identity and also to make informed decisions about voluntary disclosure of information, and using the science of privacy protection to inform policy decisions.

Potential solutions to these challenges, outlined in the PCAST report and to be considered in future cybersecurity R&D Strategic Plans, include technologies such as methods to allow agents to perform analytics on large datasets while preserving privacy and confidentiality; creating and investigating formal models of privacy that combine concepts from statistics and computer science; devising methods that give individuals knowledge of what data about them is held and appropriate control over the use of that data; exploring the privacy-preserving design of human-centered systems; creating ways to educate users about, and protect users against, actions they might take that inadvertently compromise privacy; and using the outcome of research on privacy and confidentiality protection to enable privacy- and confidentiality-related policies to be application-specific.

7. Next Steps

This review amply demonstrates the value of the research framework established in the 2011 Strategic Plan. Agencies have done a commendable job implementing the Plan, as evidenced by the ongoing research initiatives highlighted in Section 5. At this early stage, there is little need for revising the four thrusts or the set of themes specified in the strategy. However, Federal agencies should consider whether to initiate new activities directed towards the topics highlighted in Section 6.

As noted in Section 6.1, the Cyber Economic Incentives theme warrants additional emphasis. The Administration's policy for protecting the Nation's critical infrastructure is predicated upon the voluntary adoption of enhanced cybersecurity technologies, as well as voluntary participation in information sharing activities. Defining economic incentives to encourage voluntary participation is a critical aspect of this policy. The February 2013 Executive Order on "Improving Critical Infrastructure Cybersecurity"[17] explicitly promotes policies to incentivize cybersecurity. Research that informs policymakers and the private sector would be invaluable.

NITRD will work to promote the security of cyber-physical systems to support other work on critical infrastructure. These activities require collaboration between the cybersecurity community and the manufacturing and process control communities. To advance this area, the NITRD Program has established the Cyber-Physical Systems (CPS) Senior Steering Group to coordinate programs, budgets, and policy recommendations for CPS research and development.

The cybersecurity R&D strategy will evolve as our understanding of threats and counter-measures improves and matures. Factors contributing to the evolution of the strategy include improved understanding of cyber risks, scientific and engineering advancements, private sector input, legislative mandates, and Administration priorities. The NITRD Program will continue to provide a forum for the refinement of the research themes through interagency coordination groups and public-private engagements.

The principal coordination groups are the NITRD CSIA IWG, with a membership of over 100 Federal program managers and directors with responsibilities for executing cybersecurity R&D programs, and the NITRD CSIA R&D SSG, consisting of senior representatives from agencies with national cybersecurity missions. NITRD also coordinates with the SCORE IWG, which focuses on R&D for national security systems. The NITRD Program and the agencies themselves also organize workshops and conferences to maintain interactions with the research community in academia and industry.

Moving forward, the U.S. Government must continue its critical work in securing the cyber systems of today, while preparing for the threats that may emerge tomorrow. This goal is not only a formidable technical challenge, but requires fundamental shifts in the theory, design, and implementation of cyberinfrastructure to prioritize security as a critical attribute. Such a shift can only be addressed by a continuous, proactive, and comprehensive national cybersecurity R&D enterprise consisting of a healthy ecosystem of coordinated academic, Federal, and industry research. The Administration is dedicated to achieving the goal of creating a "Trustworthy Cyberspace" that both enables Federal agencies to meet their mission goals and allows all Americans to communicate, interact, and thrive in the modern digital world.

8. APPENDIX: ACRONYMS

AFOSR	Air Force Office of Scientific Research
AFRL	Air Force Research Laboratory
APP	Automatic Privacy Protection Program
ARCSYNE	Active Repositioning in Cyberspace for Synchronized Evasion Program
ARL	Army Research Laboratory

ARO	Army Research Office
ASCR	Advanced Scientific Computing Research Program
ASD (R&E)	Assistant Secretary of Defense for Research and Engineering
BAA	Broad Agency Announcement
C3I	Command, Control, Communications, and Information Systems
C4ISR	Command, Control, Communications, Computers, Intelligence, Surveillance, Reconnaissance
CEDS	Cybersecurity for Energy Delivery Systems Program
CFT	Cyber Fast Track Program
CMC	Cyber Measurement Campaign
CPS	Cyber-Physical System
CRA	Cyber Security Collaborative Research Alliance
CRASH	Clean-Slate Design of Resilient, Adaptive, Secure Hosts Program
CSIA	Cyber Security and Information Assurance
CTP	Cyber Transition to Practice
DARPA	Defense Advanced Research Projects Agency
DHS	Department of Homeland Security
DoD	Department of Defense
DoD Cyber COI	DoD Cyber S&T Community of Interest
DOE	Department of Energy
FFRDC	Federally Funded Research and Development Center
HACMS	High-Assurance Cyber Military Systems Program
HIPAA	Health Insurance Portability and Accountability Act
IARPA	Intelligence Advanced Research Projects Activity
IETF	Internet Engineering Task Force
IP	Internet Protocol
ITA	International Technology Alliance
IWG	Interagency Working Group
JSCoRE	Journal of Sensitive Cybersecurity Research and Engineering
Mobius	Model-Based Evaluation of System Dependability and Security Program
MRC	Mission-oriented Resilient Clouds Program
MURI	Multidisciplinary University Research Initiative
NCCoE	National Cybersecurity Center of Excellence
NCO	National Coordination Office

NITRD	Networking and Information Technology Research and Development
NIST	National Institute of Standards and Technology
NSA	National Security Agency
NSF	National Science Foundation
NSTC	National Science and Technology Council
NSTIC	National Strategy for Trusted Identities in Cyberspace
ODNI	Office of the Director of National Intelligence
ONC	Office of the National Coordinator for Health Information Technology
ONR	Office of Naval Research
OSD	Office of the Secretary of Defense
OSTP	Office of Science and Technology Policy
PCAST	President's Council of Advisors on Science and Technology
PI	Principal Investigator
R&D	Research and Development
S&T	Science and Technology
SaTC	Secure and Trustworthy Cyberspace Program
SBIR	Small Business Innovation Research
SCAP	Security Content Automation Protocol
SCI	Secure Coding Initiative
SCORE	Special Cyber Operations Research and Engineering
SEI	Software Engineering Institute
SFS	CyberCorps®: Scholarship for Service Program
SGCC	Smart Grid Interoperability Panel Cybersecurity Committee
SGIP-CSWG	Smart Grid Interoperability Panel-Cyber Security Working Group
SHARPS	Strategic Healthcare IT Advanced Research Projects on Security Program
SHIELD	Supply Chain Hardware Integrity for Electronics Defense Program
SPAR	Security and Privacy Assurance Research Program
SSG	Senior Steering Group
STONESOUP	Securely Taking On New Executable Software of Uncertain Provenance Program
TCIPG	Trustworthy Cyber Infrastructure for the Power

	Grid Program
THaW	Trustworthy Health and Wellness Project
TTCP	The Technical Cooperation Program
TTP	Transition To Practice Program
UARC	University Affiliated Research Center

End Notes

[1] http://www.whitehouse.gov/assets/documents/CyberspacePolicyReviewfinal.pdf.

[2] http://www.whitehouse.gov/sites/default/files/microsites/ostp/fed cybersecurity rd strategic plan 2011.pdf.

[3] http://www.nitrd.gov.

[4] http://www.gpo.gov/fdsys/pkg/FR-2013-02-19/pdf/2013-03915.pdf.

[5] http://www.whitehouse.gov/the-press-office/2013/02/12/presidential-policy-directive-critical-infrastructure-security-and-resil.

[6] http://www.nitrd.gov/pubs/2015supplement/FY2015NITRDSupplement.pdf.

[7] Submitted comments are available in their entirety at: http://www.nitrd.gov/fileupload/files/RFCSubmissionsFedCybersecurityRDStratPlan20130114.pdf.

[8] One center at Harvard University focuses on privacy issues in social science research, while the other, which is a collaboration among George Washington University, the University of California at San Diego, and the International Computer Science Institute, aims to develop an empirical basis for social-economic perspectives.

[9] http://cps-vo.org/group/mtrs.

[10] Command, Control, Communications, Computers, Intelligence, Surveillance, Reconnaissance.

[11] "Consumer Data Privacy in a Networked World: a Framework for Protecting Privacy and Promoting Innovation in the Global Digital Economy," The White House, February 2012, http://www.whitehouse.gov/sites/default/files/privacy-final.pdf.

[12] http://www.whitehouse.gov/sites/default/files/rssviewer/internationalstrategyfor cyberspace.pdf.

[13] DHS and NSF both were sponsors of these workshops, and their PIs participated. The workshop reports for these events are available at http://www.inco-trust.eu/incotrust/general/project-motivation.html.

[14] While this section outlines some cybersecurity R&D activities geared towards specific national priorities, not all end uses require specialized lines of research. Some public comments push for creation of new lines of cybersecurity research for specific end uses, such as law enforcement and defense purposes. However, the Strategic Plan already supports research on these types of areas. For example, the Tailored Trustworthy Systems theme includes having security appropriate for the transaction at hand. The Moving Target theme recognizes that additional research may be necessary to satisfy the needs of cyber law enforcement in the context of "moving" system adaptations.

[15] http://energy.gov/sites/prod/files/Energy%20Delivery%20Systems%20Cybersecurity %20 Roadmapfinalweb.pdf.

[16] http://www.whitehouse.gov/sites/default/files/microsites/ostp/pcast-nitrd2013.pdf.

[17] http://www.gpo.gov/fdsys/pkg/FR-2013-02-19/pdf/2013-03915.pdf.

INDEX

D

E

F

Q

R

S

W